CHILDREN Just Like Me

A School Like Mine

A celebration of schools around the world

DK | Penguin
Random
House

REVISED EDITION
Project editors Sam Priddy, Suneha Dutta
Project art editor Fiona Macdonald
Assistant art editor Jaileen Kaur
DTP designer Bimlesh Tiwary
Managing editors Laura Gilbert, Alka Thakur Hazarika
Managing art editors Diane Peyton Jones,
Romi Chakraborty
CTS manager Balwant Singh
Production manager Pankaj Sharma
Pre-production producer Nadine King
Producer Srijana Gurung
Art director Martin Wilson
Publisher Sarah Larter
Publishing director Sophie Mitchell
Consultant Robert Dinwiddie

FIRST EDITION
Written and edited by Penny Smith and Zahavit Shalev
Designed by Sonia Whillock-Moore
Additional editing Caroline Bingham, Elinor
Greenwood, Carrie Love, Lorrie Mack, and Fleur Star
Additional design Gemma Fletcher, Tory Gordon-
Harris, Karen Hood, Poppy Joslin, and Sadie Thomas
Publishing Manager Susan Leonard
Managing Art Editor Rachael Foster
DTP designer Ben Hung
Production Lucy Baker
Photographers Bryan Alexander, Frank Chen, Andy
Crawford, Howard Davies, George Fetting, Steve Gorton,
Minnie Pang Walker, Simon Rawles, Joginder Singh,
and Jon Spaull

First published in Great Britain in 2007
This edition published in Great Britain in 2016
by Dorling Kindersley Limited
80 Strand, London WC2R 0RL

Copyright © 2007, 2016
Dorling Kindersley Limited, London
A Penguin Random House Company
2 4 6 8 10 9 7 5 3 1
001–285261–Sept/2016

A CIP catalogue record for this book
is available from the British Library.

ISBN 978-0-2412-0736-9
Printed and bound in Hong Kong

A WORLD OF IDEAS:
SEE ALL THERE IS TO KNOW
www.dk.com

Contents

8 The Americas

10 Maria from Peru
12 Yasmin from Brazil
13 Ana from Brazil
14 Jucari from Mexico
16 Carmen from Mexico
18 Emmy from the USA
20 Ian from the USA
21 Sander from the USA
22 Lukasi from Canada

24 Africa

26 Fundi from South Africa
27 Sibusiso from South Africa
28 Safaa from Egypt
30 Semira from Ethiopia
32 Susan from Botswana

I'm Joaquin and I'm from the USA

I'm Rafael and I'm from Brazil

I'm Maria and I'm from Peru

I'm Jedidiah and I'm from Ghana

I'm Yohanna and I'm from Ethiopia

I'm Abemelek and I'm from Ethiopia

I'm Susan and I'm from Botswana

Leabharlanna Poiblí Chathair Baile Átha Cliath
Dublin City Public Libraries

34 Europe

36 Francis from England
37 Michael from Ireland
38 Anna from France
40 Alvaro and Nacho from Spain
42 Flora from Belgium
43 Isabelle from the Netherlands
44 Søren from Denmark
45 Chiara from Italy
46 Fanny from Germany
48 Marek from Poland

50 Asia

52 Ksenia from the Russia
53 Alexei from the Russia
54 Aysima from Turkey
56 Dana from Jordan
57 Yotam from Israel
58 Deepak from India
60 Sumandhara from India
61 Reena from India
62 Xinpei from China
64 Yiting from China
65 Jiyu from China
66 Hassa from Mongolia
68 Sun-Woo from South Korea
70 Momona from Japan
72 Junivio from East Timor

74 Australasia

76 Gapirri from Australia
78 Parekaawa from New Zealand

I'm Søren and I'm from Denmark

I'm Mattus and I'm from Finland

I'm Lucas and I'm from Spain

I'm Fanny and I'm from Germany

I'm Erel and I'm from Israel

I'm Shaowei and I'm from China

I'm Murk and I'm from Pakistan

I'm Mehak and I'm from India

I'm Yeh-Lin and I'm from South Korea

I'm Momona and I'm from Japan

I'm Hassa and I'm from Mongolia

I'm Parekaawa and I'm from New Zealand

A day at school

Where do children learn, who teaches them, and what do they learn about? In this book, children from Africa to Australasia show you what a typical day at school is like for them. Read through to find out how their schools are similar to yours, and also how they are different.

Off to school

Six-year-old Lucas, from Spain, goes to school in his casual clothes. He travels to school with his mother in a car. Other kids around the world walk to school, travel in school buses, or get there on their bikes. Is your school close enough to walk to, or do you use a different form of transport?

"I am at school from 9 am to 5 pm, and after that I practise sports and English."

In the class

Children use textbooks in class to find out information on lots of different topics. Some of these books contain fun activities, such as quizzes. Lots of kids also have exercise books to work in. Most children have a favourite subject. What is yours?

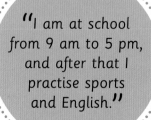

Playing sports

Yohanna and her brother, Abemelek, from Ethiopia, love to play football. Children featured in this book like to play baseball, golf, and ice hockey, while others swim or do karate. There are a lot of sports to choose from!

Meals in school

Most children get packed lunch from home or eat in the school cafeteria. Some schools provide breakfast or mid-morning meals. Fundi, from South Africa, goes to a boarding school, and both her breakfast and lunch are prepared in the school kitchen.

Teachers

Teachers are on hand to guide their students through lessons. Most schools have a different teacher for each subject. Nacho has a science teacher who encourages his interest in the subject, and teaches him new skills, such as how to use a microscope.

Learning music

Many schools have music and dance classes where children can choose to play one instrument or the other. Some kids learn music at home as well. Yeh-Lin from South Korea likes to play the clarinet, while her sisters play the flute and violin. She has performed at concerts in her school.

After school

Around the world, some children spend their evenings playing, some go to classes to learn new things, while others help out with household chores. Nine-year-old Rafael from Brazil likes to fly toy planes and play with his pet rabbit!

Homework

Children are given homework to practice things they learn at school. Fanny, from Germany, does an hour of homework and then goes out to play. How much time do you spend doing your homework?

Create your own page!
Think about what your school day is like and the things you enjoy about it.

Meet the children

Visiting schools in six continents (out of a world total of seven) has meant a lot of travelling! And at each destination children have been busily learning their languages, practising maths, and playing ball at breaktime. What's amazing is how similar schools are – and also the fascinating differences. So now it's time to meet the children from schools all around the world.

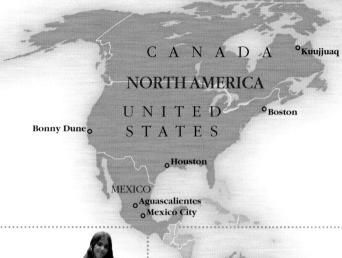

I'm Maria and I'm from Peru *I'm Yasmin and I'm from Brazil* *I'm Ana and I'm from Brazil*

From the Americas

I'm Jucari and I'm from Mexico *I'm Carmen and I'm from Mexico* *I'm Emmy and I'm from the USA* *I'm Ian and I'm from the USA* *I'm Sander and I'm from the USA* *I'm Lukasi and I'm from Canada* *I'm Dana and I'm from Jordan* *I'm Yotam and I'm from Isra...*

From Africa

I'm Fundi and I'm from South Africa *I'm Sibusiso and I'm from South Africa* *I'm Safaa and I'm from Egypt* *I'm Semira and I'm from Ethiopia* *I'm Susan and I'm from Botswana*

From Europe

I'm Francis and I'm from England *I'm Michael and I'm from Ireland*

6

I'm Gapirri and I'm
from Australia

I'm Parekaawa and
I'm from New Zealand

From Asia

I'm Alexei and
I'm from Russia

I'm Ksenia and
I'm from Russia

I'm Aysima and
I'm from Turkey

We're Deepak
and Atul and
we're from India

I'm Sumandhara
and I'm
from India

I'm Reena
and I'm
from India

I'm Xinpei and
I'm from China

I'm Jiyu and
I'm from China

I'm Yiting and
I'm from China

I'm Hassa and
I'm from
Mongolia

I'm Sun-Woo
and I'm from
South Korea

I'm Momona
and I'm from
Japan

I'm Junivio and
I'm from
East Timor

I'm Anna and I'm
from France

We're Nacho and
Alvaro and we're
from Spain

I'm Flora and I'm
from the Belguim

I'm Isabelle and
I'm from the
Netherlands

I'm Søren and I'm
from Denmark

I'm Chiara and I'm
from Italy

I'm Fanny and
I'm from
Germany

I'm Marek and
I'm from Poland

7

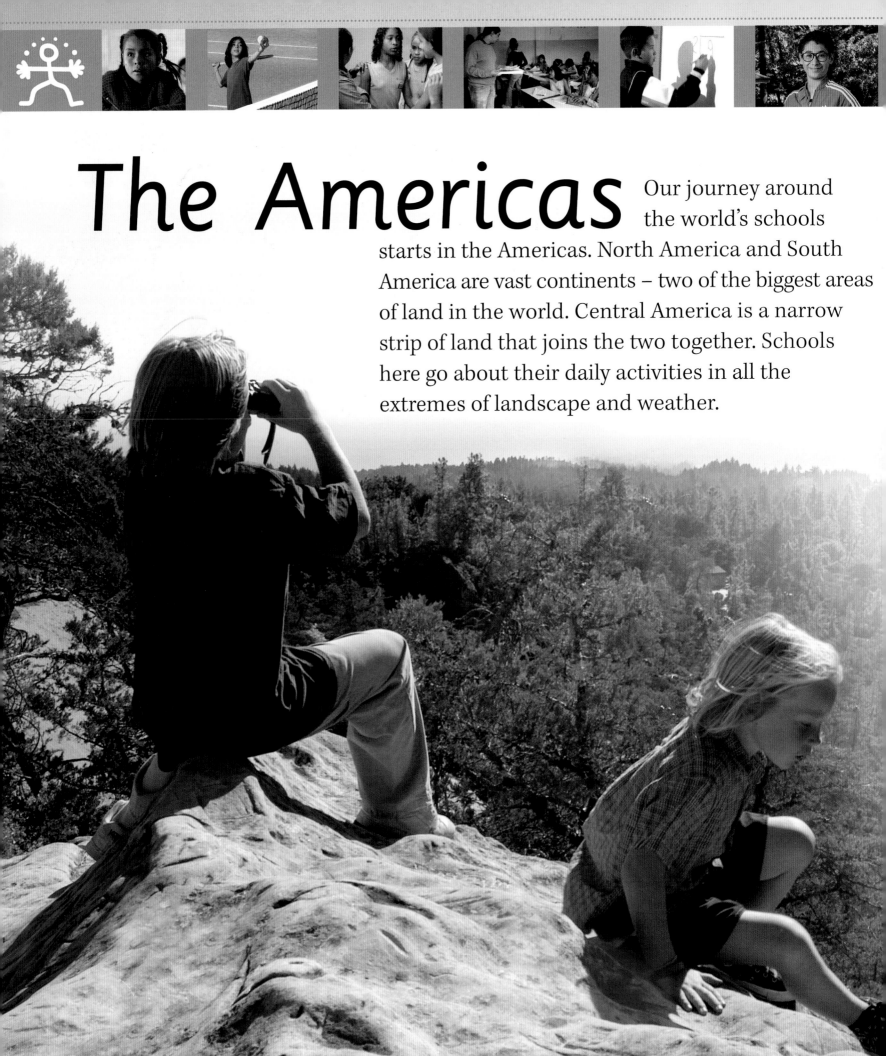

The Americas

Our journey around the world's schools starts in the Americas. North America and South America are vast continents – two of the biggest areas of land in the world. Central America is a narrow strip of land that joins the two together. Schools here go about their daily activities in all the extremes of landscape and weather.

Northern Canada

Sometimes the best way to get around Canada's far north, where the temperature can dip to as low as –40ºC (–40ºF), is by dog sleigh.

Ice hockey, Canada

Ice hockey is the top sport in Canada – and many children play it at school. Protective clothing must be worn, as players may collide (called "checking"), and the puck can travel at 160 kph (100 mph) if it's hit hard.

California, USA

Sandy beaches, snow-capped mountains, cultured cities, national parks, Hollywood, Disneyland… California has it all.

Capital city, USA

The capital city of the United States of America is Washington, D.C. – and the Capitol building is where Congress meets to pass laws and engage in other official matters.

Grand Canyon, USA

The USA has some spectacular scenery, including the colourful rocks of the Grand Canyon. In some places, the Grand Canyon is more than a mile deep.

Map labels

ALASKA (United States)

GREENLAND (To Denmark)

CANADA

NORTH AMERICA

UNITED STATES

Kuujjuaq

Boston

Bonny Dune

MEXICO

Houston

BAHAMAS

Aguascalientes
Mexico City

CUBA

HAITI

DOMINICAN REPUBLIC

JAMAICA

BELIZE
HONDURAS

GUATEMALA
EL SALVADOR

NICARAGUA

COSTA RICA

PANAMA

VENEZUELA

GUYANA

SURINAM

FRENCH GUIANA (To France)

COLOMBIA

ECUADOR

PERU

BRAZIL

SOUTH AMERICA

Huaraz

BOLIVIA

PARAGUAY

Rio de Janeiro

CHILE

ARGENTINA

URUGUAY

FALKLAND ISLANDS (To UK)

Mexico

Mexico is in North America and its official language is Spanish – there are more Spanish speakers here than in Spain. The countryside varies from desert to mountain, with beaches along both coasts.

Brazil

Brazil is the largest country in South America and home to the Amazon rainforest. Every year, in the city of Rio de Janeiro, the world-famous Rio Carnival is held.

Peru

The world's longest chain of mountains, the Andes, covers nearly half of Peru. Machu Picchu (left), an ancient ruined city of the Incas, is situated high up in the peaks. Many different native peoples live in Peru, both in the Andes and in the Amazon Basin, which covers the rest of the country.

Maria from Peru

Maria lives in Pampacancha, a village in the Andes region of Peru. Most people here live off the food they grow. Maria's parents are separated. Her mother lives and works in the town of Huaraz, 50 km (30 miles) away.

Pampacancha nestles in the Cordillera Negra – the black mountains – where rain and snow rarely fall.

This gorgeous puppy doesn't yet have a name.

Family

Maria and her brother Eliseo live with their grandmother, two aunts, an uncle, and two young cousins.

Education for everyone

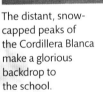

The government is encouraging rural families to keep their children at school rather than use them for farm work. This mural at Maria's school says: "Girls and boys have the right to study".

The distant, snow-capped peaks of the Cordillera Blanca make a glorious backdrop to the school.

At 10, Maria is older than the rest of her class because she is making up the year of school she missed when she lived in Huaraz with her mother.

Languages

Maria has copied out the words of a Quechua-language song. Schools in Peru used to teach only in Spanish, but Quechua children often couldn't keep up and would drop out. Now children learn in both languages.

Wara

Trousers

ruripa

Skirt

Warmipa Tsukun

Man's hat

Ullqupa Tsu

Woman's ha

A bite to eat

At mid-morning break, the children are given soya milk and fortified bread (bread with added vitamins), provided by the government. This is their first meal of the day.

A close-up look at a chicken in a nature lesson

"Today I used a computer for the first time. It was exciting! The computer uses Spanish, but normally we use Quechua in class."

Outdoor lessons

Sometimes the teacher takes the class outside for a nature lesson. This is a chance to learn practical things, such as how to plant and tend crops, or the best way to care for the domestic animals like sheep, cows, and hens that people rely on.

There's no sports equipment, but the children play games such as tug-of-war, and take part in wheelbarrow races.

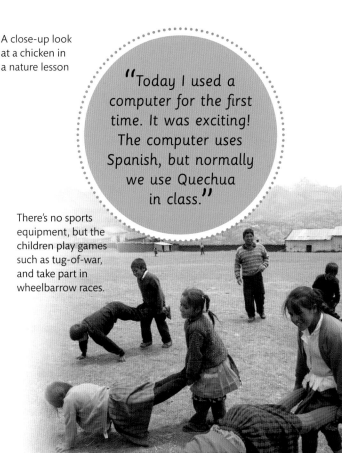

Fortified bread

Food is one good reason why children attend school.

Everyone crowds around one of the school's desktop computers. Some basic laptops have also recently been supplied to the school.

Helping out

After school, Maria and Eliseo help their grandmother to pick wheat for the main meal. They then use the water from this standpipe to wash the wheat and remove the chaff. Later, Maria helps her aunt to do some laundry.

Yasmin from Brazil

Eleven-year-old Yasmin lives in a poor neighbourhood of Rio de Janeiro. There are 32 children in her class and not enough teachers to go around. The students only have very limited access to computers.

School days

Lessons start at 7:30 am and usually end at noon, but sometimes Yasmin has to go home early if there is no teacher for her class.

Family life

Yasmin has four brothers and three sisters. The children's grandmother looks after them while their mother is at work.

Yasmin and her mother share a love of teddy bears.

Making learning fun

A 15-year-old student at the school reads a story to Yasmin's class. The aim of these lessons is to encourage the children's interest in reading.

> "My favourite lesson is English. It's important to speak other languages."

Yasmin really enjoys her drumming class. They play a kind of Brazilian music called samba. Huge groups of hundreds of drummers perform at the Rio Carnival.

Today's lunch is pasta and sausages.

Lunchtime

A free meal is provided for the children. Usually it's beans and rice, chicken with potatoes, or pasta and sausages.

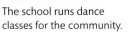

The school runs dance classes for the community.

Yasmin plays in the courtyard outside her home.

Yasmin and her sister wash the dishes after lunch.

Ana from Brazil

Ana also lives in Rio. Her favourite subject is history. Every Thursday at her school the children do two hours of sport. They go on regular trips to museums and even abroad.

Ana is an only child. She lives in an apartment with her parents.

The journey to school takes about half an hour on the bus.

Helping others

Ana is fortunate to attend a spacious school. Pupils there raise money for a centre that provides poor children with a place to study, eat a hot meal, and sleep. Twice a year they visit the centre to play with the children who use it.

> "I hope to go to the best university and become a fashion journalist."

Ana goes to regular street-dancing lessons. She has been attending classes since she was five and although she still enjoys them, she's starting to get a little bored now.

Learning with computers

The school is well equipped with computers. The students use them a great deal for lessons and tests.

Ana's English language textbook

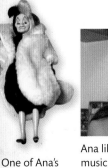

One of Ana's ceramic dolls

Ana likes listening to music, especially Mexican pop groups.

After she does her homework, Ana surfs the net on the computer in her bedroom.

Ana and her mother chat in the kitchen. The family has a maid to do the cleaning.

13

Jucari *from* Mexico

Jucari, who is ten, lives with his mother, father, and six-year-old sister in a residential area of Mexico City. His family were originally Purepecha Indians, and his name means "great wise one" in their language. Jucari goes to a large public school in the centre of the city.

"I would like to be an archaeologist and study old temples."

Jucari says goodbye to his mother at the school gates. Although his journey should take about an hour, it takes twice as long when the traffic is very heavy.

School life

The school's courtyard provides a big, safe place for Jucari and his friends to play before lessons and at breaktime. The boys and girls at their school all wear a comfortable blue and white uniform and trainers.

Daily lessons

Jucari pays attention during maths lessons, but his favourite subject is history. There are 36 children in his class, and their teacher is Fernando Miranda. They call him *maestro* Fernando.

Jucari chose his desk because it is close to both the blackboard and the interactive whiteboard. There are plenty of computers in the school, and Jucari enjoys using them.

Jucari's exercise book is full of cars.

This is his maths book.

Day of the Dead

In Mexico, the Day of the Dead is an important celebration. On this day, people ask the spirits to look after them in their everyday life. Jucari places an offering of sweets on the school altar before a portrait of Benito Juárez, a Mexican president who fought to ensure a school place for every child.

Papier-mâché skeleton

Ceremonial sculpture

Skull sculpture

All the children at Jucari's school make special artworks or write poems as part of the celebrations. *Dia de Muertos* means Day of the Dead in Spanish.

After school

With his mother, Jucari takes the Metro home from school. Then they take the car or catch the bus, to either his house or to the sweet shop his mother owns.

Jucari and his mother squeeze on to a rush-hour train. Every day he gets homework, which he carries in his rucksack.

Jucari and his sister often eat at their grandfather's. His tailoring business is next door to their mother's sweet shop.

Jucari sleeps in a racing-car bed. He loves racing cars, but he doesn't want to drive one because they're dangerous.

Breaktime

Jucari's favourite playground game is Tazos™, which is played with tokens found in packets of crisps and snacks. Each player puts a token on the ground, then his opponents try to flip it over with their own tokens. Whoever succeeds keeps both tokens.

Children can't buy Tazos™ in shops – they have to collect them from crisp packets or win them from their friends.

School sports

Jucari enjoys lots of sports at school, including track events, basketball, football, swimming, and handball. He is on the school handball team.

Jucari and his sister have a cat, and it's Jucari's job to feed it and clean its box.

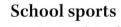

The school has its own outdoor swimming pool.

Carmen from Mexico

Carmen is the youngest of 14 children, whose ages range from 36 down to 10. She lives in a tiny village in the state of Aguascalientes, in Mexico. The school she goes to has just nine pupils. They are all taught together by their teacher, Michaela, who recently left secondary school.

Carmen and her mother walking near their home with one of Carmen's nieces and one of her nephews. Large families are fairly common, though becoming rarer, in rural areas of Mexico.

The school

The building on the left was the schoolroom until the new building on the right was built.

Carmen's model of a traditional Mexican house

Carmen's favourite teddy bear

Carmen is seen posing here with her class. Their teacher is at the back with "16" on her top.

Children attend school from 8 am to 1:30 pm, Monday to Friday. Maria does 30 minutes of homework each day, too.

Carmen's notebook

"Sometimes we get science experiments to do at home using things like plants, nails, oil, salt and matches."

Children's art decorates the school walls.

16

Herb garden

The children grow herbs in the school yard. People here grow much of their food, and children are expected to help.

Textbooks

The Mexican government supplies small rural schools with textbooks designed for children learning in mixed-age groups. Carmen works through her book at her own pace with help from the teacher.

Carmen and one of her classmates doing a maths exercise outside their school. Their teacher works hard to make learning active and fun.

Rota of jobs done by the children

Chores

The children take an active role in looking after their school. Every child has a different job each day, such as collecting water or mopping the floor, as Carmen is doing here.

Field trip

Carmen loves natural sciences because this class offers an opportunity to go out and explore. In fact, a great deal of learning takes place outside the classroom. The children have interviewed local elderly people and visited the river to learn about caring for the environment.

Making meals

There are no local shops. Instead, a truck comes round selling fruit and vegetables to the villagers.

Carmen helps her mother cook a typical dinner – noodle soup with tomatoes, onions, and peppers, accompanied by a chilli salsa and maize tortillas.

Afterwards, Carmen does the washing up using a large bucket, which she fills from the tap outside the house.

Carmen plays at being a school teacher with her nephew

Emmy from the USA

Nine-year-old Emmy lives very close to her school in a suburb of Houston, Texas. She likes to cycle to school – a journey of about three minutes – but she sometimes takes the bus. Emmy's school helps the local community. At Christmas, the school arranges for the children to take gifts, clothes, and food to low-income families.

Houston is the fourth most populous city in the USA. The city is home to the Lyndon B. Johnson Space Centre, which controls NASA's space exploration missions from Earth.

The neighbourhood

There is plenty of land where Emmy lives, so the family home has a front and rear garden. This is a very friendly community. Emmy spends her free time with her friends at the neighbourhood pool and playground. Every year the local families get together to organize a street party.

Emmy with her parents, brother Andrew, and sister, Caroline

The sign on Emmy's bedroom door

Caroline & Emmy's Room

Soccer Princess

Sharing a room

Emmy shares a room with her older sister Caroline, who is 12. One wall is almost completely covered with photographs of the girls' friends.

The wall of photos in the girls' bedroom

Emmy was in kindergarten when she drew this picture of her mother.

Flying the flag

The school's flagpole displays two flags – the flag of the United States, nicknamed the "Stars and Stripes", and the state flag for Texas, called the "Lone Star Flag". Every morning there is a short ceremony by the flagpole and the children say a pledge of allegiance to both flags.

Emmy's school is on the same street as her home. This is the yard inside the school gates at the front of the school.

There is a large space at the back of the school for breaktime, with plenty of trees to provide shade during the hot summer months.

Church

Emmy's family are Greek Orthodox Christians. Houston is home to one of the biggest Greek Orthodox communities in the USA. Every October the community hosts the "Original Greek Festival" – three days of Greek food, music, and dance. It has been a regular event in Houston for the past 40 years.

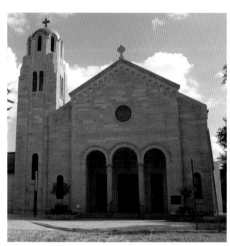

Class trips

There are 20 children in Emmy's class, made up of an equal number of girls and boys. Last year they saw a production at the Houston Ballet. This year, they are looking forward to a bus trip to visit the state capital, Austin. Emmy started here at the age of four and will go to middle school when she is 11.

In the classroom, Emmy sits at one of five desks pushed together.

Emmy draws flowers in her art class.

There is no uniform, but the school does not allow strappy tops or very short shorts.

Keen sportswoman

Emmy swims competitively and would like to be a professional swimmer when she grows up. She and her friends play kick ball and four square in the school playground, and she also plays basketball, softball, and volleyball out of school.

A school day

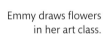

The school day runs from 8 am to 3 pm, Monday to Friday. All the lessons are in English. Emmy loves learning in groups and using the computer. Her least favourite subjects are music and maths.

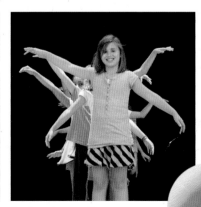

The school has a computer lab and there are also computers in some of the classrooms.

Emmy rehearses for a performance of the ballet *The Nutcracker*.

At break, Emmy and her friends play a game called four square.

Emmy plays sport through the church and various youth leagues.

Ian from the USA

Ian lives in Boston. Most days his dad gives him a lift to school in the car, which takes about 10 minutes, but sometimes he walks with his mum. He likes everything about his school.

On his journey to school, Ian likes to look out for children he knows from a local high school, where his dad is the athletics director.

Ian is an only child.

He plays a great deal of sport.

Baseball

Ian loves sports, and would like to become a professional baseball player. His bedroom is full of sporting memorabilia, but there is still room for his pet guinea pig's cage.

Baseball trophy

This is Peanut, Ian's pet guinea pig.

Ian is an accomplished pianist and takes lessons at the Community Music Centre. His father plays in a heavy metal band.

School days

School runs from 8 am to 3:15 pm, Monday to Friday. Ian is now 10, and he started here when he was six. He'll be 12 when he leaves.

In the classroom

There are 17 children in Ian's class. Ian likes to sit in the middle of the room facing the door, but he doesn't sit in the same place every day.

This is an illustrated story Ian wrote himself.

Lunchtime

Everybody brings a packed lunch. Ian's mother makes his and then checks if it's OK with him. It always is!

Some children play soccer in the school playground, while others sit on the sidelines and cheer them on.

Sander from the USA

Sander is 11 and lives in Bonny Dune, California. He spends three days a week being homeschooled by his parents, with his brother, Olin, and two days a week at school. Sander likes learning at his own pace.

Feeding the chickens and collecting their eggs is Sander's job.

The boys and their father make a picture to celebrate Halloween. Later, Sander does some violin practice. Sander's parents take turns to teach Sander and Olin.

Sander's exercise book

Nature report

Sander chose this Ponderosa Pine for his nature report. He and his dad used a special tool to cut a tiny core out of the tree to help them calculate its age.

The tree rings suggest that this pine is around 300 to 400 years old.

Baseball dreams

Sander plays in a baseball league during the autumn and winter. He would love to become a professional player.

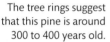

Baseball trophy

A glove worn by Alex Rodriguez of the New York Yankees

Sander owns a signed baseball.

At school, the children don't sit at desks but around tables. There are different work stations for each subject.

The boys are baking a pumpkin pie as part of a cooking lesson with their father.

The forest is a few minutes drive away.

Free time

California's climate is mild, so Sander spends a lot of time playing outdoors.

Sander loves skateboarding and skates whenever he can.

The boys play in a treehouse that Sander made.

Sander dug this fort, which is deep enough to stand in.

Tubbs, the family cat

Getting to school

Lukasi lives close to his school, so it's rare for him to stay home because of bad weather. He can walk to school in 10 minutes. He often meets dogs along the way that he likes to stop and stroke.

Most children travel into school on the school bus. It makes a circuit of about 8 km (5 miles) to pick everybody up. Occasionally school is cancelled because of a storm, but it is never closed because of cold weather.

"I like to learn from computers, and I like maths. My favourite subject is gym."

Lukasi is very sporty. Here he is playing dodgeball with the kids in his class. Lukasi also plays soccer, tennis, and badminton.

The view from Lukasi's classroom

A plaque in traditional Inuit style

My class

There are 18 children in Lukasi's class – 5 boys and 13 girls – and their ages range from 8 to 12. They don't have to wear a school uniform. Each child sits at his or her own desk.

Lukasi makes notes about an experiment he is doing in science class. His homework will be about the experiment.

Karate class

Lukasi has been doing karate since he was seven years old. About 25 children in Kuujjuaq attend karate lessons twice a week. Lukasi likes karate, but his favourite hobbies are hunting, fishing, and trapping.

Waiting to begin

Doing stretches to warm up

Preparing for a high kick!

With help from his grandfather, Lukasi makes a Samurai sword out of wood. His grandfather ordered the wood from Montreal and it arrived by ship in the summer. Over the years they have made model medieval swords and shields as well as hunting rifles together.

Africa

This is the second-largest of the world's continents (after Asia) and home to 1.1 billion people. Seventy-five per cent of children in sub-Saharan Africa receive a primary school education, and governments are working hard to provide schooling for everyone.

This is Africa

Egypt

Egypt, in the northeast of Africa, is where some of the earliest schools existed as long as 5,000 years ago. This land of ancient wonders is home to the pyramids.

Ethiopia

Ethiopia is one of the oldest nations in the world, and unlike most other African countries, it managed, largely, to avoid European colonization. At least 70 languages are spoken in Ethiopia, but English is the main foreign language as it is the one teachers use in secondary schools.

MOROCCO
WESTERN SAHARA (Occupied by Morocco)
TUNISIA
ALGERIA
LIBYA
EGYPT
○ Cairo

AFRICA

MAURITANIA
MALI
NIGER
CHAD
SUDAN
ERITREA
DJIBOUTI
SENEGAL
GAMBIA
GUINEA-BISSAU
GUINEA
BURKINA FASO
BENIN
NIGERIA
SIERRA LEONE
LIBERIA
CÔTE D'IVOIRE
GHANA
TOGO
CAMEROON
CENTRAL AFRICAN REPUBLIC
SOUTH SUDAN
ETHIOPIA
○ Addis Ababa
SOMALIA
EQUATORIAL GUINEA
GABON
CONGO
DEMOCRATIC REPUBLIC OF THE CONGO
UGANDA
RWANDA
BURUNDI
KENYA
TANZANIA
ANGOLA
ZAMBIA
MALAWI
MOZAMBIQUE
MADAGASCAR
NAMIBIA
ZIMBABWE
BOTSWANA
○ Molepolole
SWAZILAND
SOUTH AFRICA
LESOTHO
○ Richmond

Botswana

Botswana is landlocked, and despite the Kalahari Desert in the west, it is a haven for wildlife. Crocodiles, buffalo, wildebeest, lions, hippos, rhinos, giraffes, and the African elephant are all found here.

South African landscape

The South African landscape varies from the dry Karoo interior to the many gardens and vineyards of the Cape. Cape Town, the capital (shown here), sits below the spectacular cliffs of the flat-topped Table Mountain, here shrouded in cloud, nicknamed the "tablecloth".

Wildlife in South Africa

South Africa is home to the "big five" – buffalo, elephant, leopard, lion, and rhino. The coastal waters teem with sea creatures, and a huge variety of birds, including jackass penguins, make their home here.

Fundi from South Africa

Fundi is 12 years old and goes to boarding school in Richmond, in the Kwazulu-Natal province of South Africa. She spends three weeks at a time there, then goes home to see her family.

In summer, Fundi wears a navy blue-and-white dress. In winter she wears a navy suit.

"My hero is Nelson Mandela, first president of the new South Africa."

Nelson Mandela fought against apartheid, which separated people because of their race.

Fundi wears white socks in summer and navy socks in winter.

Pietermaritzburg

Fundi's school is spread over sloping hills on the outskirts of Richmond town. Nearby is the city of Pietermaritzburg where many students from Fundi's school will go to high school.

Start the day

Fundi wakes up at 6 am and has eggs and traditional porridge for breakfast. She usually wears school uniform, but on Market Day she can wear her own clothes.

The school system

Fundi has a different teacher for each subject and she likes them all. This is Miss Mkhize who teaches Zulu and netball. There are 27 children in Fundi's class and almost half of them are boarders.

School sports

Fundi plays sport most days. Her school has a swimming pool and she likes swimming there, even in chilly weather. Fundi is in the school swimming squad. The school also teaches cricket and football, but only the boys do these.

Fundi is good at netball. She is in the school team, which competes against other schools.

On Market Day, Fundi and her friends sell food they have made themselves as part of their school work. They have to keep track of costs so they can make a profit when they sell the food.

After school, Fundi and her friends meet at a bench in the school grounds. It's their chance to catch up and share stories. Fundi likes having boys in her school because she thinks they are fun.

Dormitory life

Fundi shares a dormitory with nine other girls. They are not allowed to talk after lights out at 8:30 pm and sometimes Fundi finds it hard to go straight to sleep.

In the computer room, children play games, make spreadsheets, and learn how to type.

Sibusiso from South Africa

Eleven-year-old Sibusiso lives on a strawberry farm outside Richmond, in South Africa. His home is 8 km (5 miles) from school and each day it takes him over an hour to walk there.

The long walk

Although it is tiring, Sibusiso doesn't mind the walk to school. He is on his own for half the journey, then he meets friends and they walk the rest of the way together.

A working day

When Sibusiso leaves for school, his father goes to work on the farm and his mother sets off to her job in the farm owner's kitchen.

Sibusiso's parents work on a strawberry farm like this one.

To keep safe, children walk in single file by the road. The child in front carries a flag.

Sibusiso drew this picture of the farm owner's house. This is where he goes to watch television.

School age

There are 23 children in Sibusiso's class. They are mostly the same age as Sibusiso, although some, who missed out on their early education, are aged up to 15.

Sibusiso tries to keep his maths book neat.

Sibusiso's school bag is a rucksack that he carries on his back.

Classrooms open onto the playground. Sometimes the children have an outdoor assembly on the grass.

Miss Priscilla Reddy is the headmistress.

Children grow plants in the school garden. It is fenced with barbed wire to keep robbers out of the school buildings.

This sign is on the library door. Its message is that the school does not support violence of any kind.

School lunch

Sibusiso enjoys the food that is cooked at school. Like the other children, he washes and dries his plate after the meal.

Rice and stew is a typical school meal.

The cook serves food from the veranda of her house.

The children eat lunch on benches outside their classrooms.

Safaa from Egypt

Cairo

Cairo and the area around it is home to more than 16 million people. Many tourists visit the city, particularly the 4,500-year-old pyramids.

Ten-year-old Safaa lives in Abu Sir, a neighbourhood about 15 km (10 miles) from the centre of Cairo, the capital of Egypt. She is the youngest of six children – three girls and three boys. Safaa's father works on archaeological digs and as a tour guide, and her mother sells goods in the local market.

Safaa

School building

Safaa's school has a small, secure garden. The school is free to attend and all the girls consider themselves very lucky to go there because their families could not afford the costs of uniforms and travel at other schools.

Walking to school

It takes Safaa just 15 minutes to walk to school with her sister Yasmine and their friend Hanaa. Sometimes they buy a snack on the way. The school day runs from 8 am to 1 pm, Saturday to Wednesday. The building is open some of the time during the summer holidays for girls who need to catch up on work or who want to use the library.

Egyptian girls and women often wear headscarves as part of their cultural tradition, but the practice varies from family to family. There are no men or boys in school, so the girls sometimes take their scarves off.

Man selling bread on the streets of Abu Sir

The garden

Here, in the courtyard of the school's garden, the girls discuss a topic – urban pollution – without the teachers being present. Sometimes they also get projects to go off and research independently. This kind of active learning is very popular with the students.

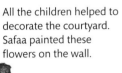

All the children helped to decorate the courtyard. Safaa painted these flowers on the wall.

Safaa's favourite subject is Arabic. These are colourful signs in Arabic and English.

The classroom

There are 36 girls in the school aged 7 to 14, with a further 20 on the waiting list. They are all taught in one big classroom by their two teachers, who they call "miss". Girls who misbehave are made to stand apart and are not allowed to participate in the lesson.

Everybody enjoys skipping.

There's no organized sport, but the girls love to run around and play in the school's garden.

Fun classroom games help develop the girls' co-ordination.

Safaa and her friends take part in a role-play activity. Safaa plays the part of a son in a family that has just found out they are being given money to start a business.

Mask depicting the father

Time to eat

At mid-morning, lessons stop so the girls can eat. Safaa eats a typical Egyptian breakfast, which consists of pitta bread, falafel (deep-fried chickpea balls), and *ful medames* (broad or fava beans).

Falafel

Pitta

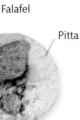

Beans

"My teacher is my favourite person. My greatest wish is to complete my studies and go to a teacher training college."

Tonight is a homework night. The girls don't get homework every night, but they have regular tests to make sure they are keeping up. Safaa looks over her task with Yasmine and their father.

29

Semira from Ethiopia

Semira is 12 years old and lives in a children's home in Addis Ababa, the capital of Ethiopia. Some of the children at the home are orphans who lost their parents to a disease called AIDS. Semira and her friends go to a large state school that has more than 2,500 students.

The country

Ethiopia is an agricultural country – it's Africa's biggest exporter of coffee. However, sometimes there is not enough rainfall, so crops fail and people do not have enough food to eat. Less than half the population can read and write.

Children at the home are enthusiastic readers. Here they are unloading a donation of books from the USA.

Good health

The home is run by three adults and the children refer to them as their "parents". It also has its own nurse. She makes sure the children are healthy and gives them medicine when they need it. Semira is a Muslim and chooses to wear a headscarf to school. This is a Muslim sign of modesty.

School is 30 minutes' walk from the home. The children walk together, the older ones looking after the little ones.

Semira wants people to understand what it is like to grow up in Ethiopia. She is writing a book about her experiences.

Home life

There are 14 children in Semira's home and she enjoys living with so many children. She shares a dormitory with seven other girls. At night they leave the light on because the younger ones are afraid of the dark.

Semira helps to make traditional Ethiopian bread, called *injera*.

The home's weekly shop includes lots of fresh vegetables.

Injera is used to scoop up food or as an edible plate.

In class

Semira has nine different subjects, each with a different teacher. There are more than 50 students in her class. Semira first went to school when she was five, but some of her classmates started school later and these children are now 15 years old.

Semira's school

Semira sits with her friends to eat lunch.

Lunchtime

Semira and her friends take packed lunches to school. Today's lunch is rice and vegetables. This was prepared by the home's cook, who makes healthy, largely vegetarian, dishes.

"I saw a programme about an early human skeleton called Lucy. I'd like to be an archaeologist and discover the next one.**"**

The lessons

Semira's favourite subject is maths because she thinks the teacher is very good. She also likes biology and would like to study science when she is older. Teaching is mostly done from the blackboard as there is not enough room to work in small groups.

Susan from Botswana

Susan is nine and lives in a village in southeast Botswana. As both her parents have died, Susan is looked after by her grandmother. Susan goes to school in the sprawling town of Molepolole, then to an after-school club for orphans and children whose parents need help looking after them.

Susan's schoo

Susan's school is close to her home and it takes only a few minutes to walk there. She starts at 7:30 am and finishes at 12:30 pm. During the day the students are given a snack of bread and milk.

Although Botswana is more than twice the size of the UK, only about two million people live there. That is about the number of people who live in a large European city.

The roof is made of straw (called thatch) held in place by ribbons. On some huts these are brightly coloured.

In Susan's village, mud huts sit alongside buildings made from bricks. Cooking is usually done on a stove outside. Susan likes living with her grandmother and thinks she is very kind.

The huts have no running water, so villagers have to carry buckets of water from the well nearby.

Susan's older brother and two sisters also live with their grandmother. One of Susan's sisters has a baby of her own.

Class time

There are 31 boys and girls in Susan's class. Their teacher is Miss Reetsand and Susan calls her "teacher". Miss Reetsand is Susan's hero – Susan thinks she is very beautiful.

Susan and her friends wear grey uniforms to school.

Children take turns to write answers on the blackboard.

Written work

Susan is taught in English and the national language, Setswana. Her favourite subjects are English and maths.

Susan has written in her workbook in Setswana.

After-school club

After school, Susan goes to a day-care centre for orphans, where more than 400 children are looked after each day. Here she can talk freely to counsellors, who help her cope without parents.

This book is used by Susan in her social studies class.

Susan has decorated her pencil case with a picture of the footballer Khumo Motlhabane.

"I hope that one day I can be a nurse and help people who are ill and make them well."

Susan eats dinner at the day-care centre and helps to wash up afterwards.

Bible reading

At the day-care centre, Susan has classes in Bible studies. Teachers at the centre also help Susan with her school homework as Susan finds this difficult.

Europe

This continent stretches from the cold lands north of the Arctic Circle to the warm and sunny countries of Spain and Greece. In Europe, education in schools has been part of a tradition lasting thousands of years and Europe is home to some of the world's oldest schools and universities.

This is Europe

Denmark

The capital city of Denmark is Copenhagen. This sea-facing city is home to Queen Margrethe, from the oldest royal family in Europe.

The Netherlands

Much of the Netherlands lies below sea level and its windmills are used to help keep the country from flooding. The Netherlands is the world's biggest exporter of cut flowers and bulbs.

Belgium

The Atomium monument (below) is in Brussels, Belgium's capital city. Belgium has three official languages: Dutch, French, and German.

Ireland

Often called the Emerald Isle because of its green pastures, Ireland has a long tradition of music, dance, and poetry.

England

England is part of the United Kingdom, which also includes Wales, Scotland, and Northern Ireland. London is the capital and one of the biggest cities in Europe.

ICELAND

NORWAY
SWEDEN
FINLAND

Saint Petersburg

ESTONIA

RUSSIA

Moscow

LATVIA

UNITED KINGDOM

Tullydonnell

IRELAND

DENMARK
Vejen

LITHUANIA

KALININGRAD (RUSSIA)

London

Amsterdam
NETHERLANDS

Brussels
BELGIUM
GERMANY
LUXEMBOURG
Paris

FRANCE
E   U   R   O   P   E

POLAND

BELARUS

UKRAINE

CZECH REPUBLIC
Kraków

Schwabhausen

SLOVAKIA

AUSTRIA
HUNGARY

MOLDOVA

SWITZERLAND

SLOVENIA
Milan

PORTUGAL

SPAIN
Madrid

ANDORRA

ITALY

CROATIA
SAN MARINO
BOSNIA & HERZEGOVINA
SERBIA

ROMANIA

MONTENEGRO
KOSOVO

BULGARIA

ALBANIA
MACEDONIA

GREECE

Istanbul
TURKEY

Poland

Kraków, Poland's former capital, is a major cultural centre. It is home to Jagiellonian University, Poland's oldest and most prestigious university.

Spain

Spain is a vast and varied country, with differing languages, cultures, and traditions, region to region. Flamenco dancing is a southern speciality.

France

France is the most visited country in the world. The Eiffel Tower dominates the skyline in the capital city, Paris. The tower receives almost seven million visitors each year.

Germany

Germany has a wealth of history and landscapes – from fairytale castles, like Neuschwanstein (shown here), to forests and Bavarian mountains.

Italy

Because of its shape, Italians fondly refer to their country as *Lo Stivale* (the boot). It is composed of many states, which were only unified into one country in 1861.

Francis from England

Francis is nine years old and lives in London with his parents, two sisters, and one brother. Francis and both of his sisters go to the same school. They walk there, often meeting friends along the way.

Children wear navy trousers, shorts, or skirts with the school sweatshirt. Girls also have the option of a blue-and-white checked dress in the summer.

Classroom

There are 30 children in Francis's class. Their teacher is Mr Brady. Each classroom has a whiteboard, which the teacher can write on. It is also linked to a computer so it can be used to show pictures, charts, and films.

There is a school canteen, but Francis brings a packed lunch. He always has some fruit.

Assembly

Each assembly has a theme. Today, Francis's year group has gathered for an assembly about St George, the patron saint of England. They are using songbooks to sing a song about him.

This model bird is part of a project about birds.

Bird project

This is the nesting box that Francis has made.

The class is making nesting boxes. These will be hung from trees in the school grounds to attract small birds.

In this activity, the children are playing at being a footballer and a TV interviewer. Francis is using a rolled-up piece of paper as a pretend microphone.

Francis is learning to play the guitar. He tries to practise every evening.

On summer evenings, when the weather allows, Francis plays cricket in his garden.

With his dad, Francis carries the recycling box to the pavement for collection.

Michael from Ireland

Michael lives in Tullydonnell in County Louth, about 50 km (30 miles) north of Dublin. He goes to the local school, where there are about 120 pupils. His favourite playground games are football and pretend wrestling.

School is only two fields away from Michael's home. Michael started coming here when he was five, although some children start when they are four or six. He has lots of friends, some from his own school, and some from other local schools who he met when his father ran a pub.

School bus

About 50 children can travel in this bus on special outings. Michael likes looking out for castles on the journey.

Classroom

The 28 children of Year Two and Year Three share a classroom. They have two teachers. Mrs McKeown teaches mostly in Irish, and Miss Boylan in English.

Michael likes to sit near the front of the class.

Learning Gaelic

The children spend half their time at school learning Irish Gaelic. Michael says this is his least favourite subject, although he is quite good at it.

Nature lesson

The children are planting bulbs. They have been learning about different trees and plants, and are also using what they have learnt in their art lessons.

Michael's family

Michael, who is eight years old, is the oldest of five children. His sister Roisin is six, twins Katie and Patrick are four, and Cormac is six months.

The class travels to the local swimming pool once a week for swimming lessons.

Michael's classmates standing by a brightly coloured mural on the playground wall.

Michael is good at football and spends a lot of time practising.

Anna from France

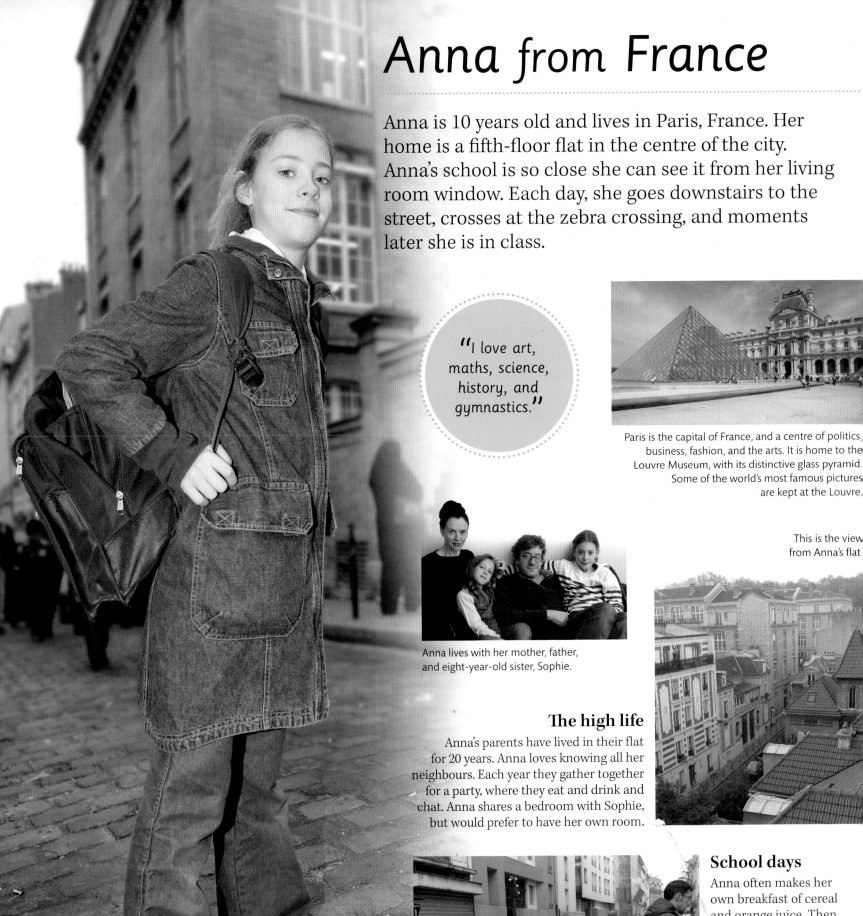

Anna is 10 years old and lives in Paris, France. Her home is a fifth-floor flat in the centre of the city. Anna's school is so close she can see it from her living room window. Each day, she goes downstairs to the street, crosses at the zebra crossing, and moments later she is in class.

"I love art, maths, science, history, and gymnastics."

Paris is the capital of France, and a centre of politics, business, fashion, and the arts. It is home to the Louvre Museum, with its distinctive glass pyramid. Some of the world's most famous pictures are kept at the Louvre.

This is the view from Anna's flat.

Anna lives with her mother, father, and eight-year-old sister, Sophie.

The high life

Anna's parents have lived in their flat for 20 years. Anna loves knowing all her neighbours. Each year they gather together for a party, where they eat and drink and chat. Anna shares a bedroom with Sophie, but would prefer to have her own room.

School days

Anna often makes her own breakfast of cereal and orange juice. Then she walks to school with Sophie. On most days of the week, the school day lasts from 8.30 am to 4 pm, including five hours of classes. However, on Wednesdays there are only classes in the morning.

n class

here are 24 children in Anna's class. At the eginning of each school year, the shops get crowded ith children buying *les fournitures scolaires* – a long st of materials they need for each of their classes, cluding pens, pencils, and notebooks.

Anna's favourite subject is art. This is one of her paintings.

Sometimes Anna has tests at school. She doesn't mind being tested but she likes to get good results. She is also making a magazine of her recent 10-day school trip to the mountains, where she skied and visited caves.

This playground can be seen from the school building. It is for little children.

Lunchtime

Children have an hour and a half for lunch, which they eat in the school canteen. Anna would prefer to take packed lunches to school, but children are not usually allowed to do this in France.

Anna has chosen rice salad, bread, chicken, beans, pineapple, and yoghurt.

Playground fun

There are three playgrounds at Anna's school. Anna and her friends like to play catch. When it is cold, they stay inside and read in the library.

Home time

nna spends about an hour each evening on her omework. She works at a desk in her bedroom. After e finishes, she reads and plays with Sophie and their nimal toys. These are kept in their own little house n a shelf. The animals' feet are magnetic so they can tick to a metal surface such as a fridge.

Anna has had guitar lessons for two years. These are strict and she has to pass exams each year to be able to continue.

Alvaro and Nacho *from* Spain

Alvaro

Nacho

Many people who live in Torrelodones travel into Madrid, the capital of Spain, to work.

Ten-year-old twins Alvaro and Nacho live in Torrelodones, 20 km (13 miles) northwest of Madrid. Their mother drives them and their two cousins to school every day. The boys are in different classes, but they both like science and dislike languages.

At home

The boys live with their parents. The family has a housekeeper named Maria, but she does not live with them.

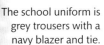

The twins eat breakfast with their father before leaving for school in the car.

The school uniform is grey trousers with a navy blazer and tie.

Many children find it more comfortable to use trolleys rather than backpacks to carry their schoolbooks.

School building

Spanish summers can be extremely hot, so the school was designed with the heat in mind. Special blinds keep the sun out while allowing the air to circulate.

Art class

Each child has their own desk, but for art lessons the desks are pushed together so eight or ten children can work in a group.

Alvaro holds up his picture.

Science class

The teacher shows Nacho how to use a microscope during a science lesson. Nacho says he is interested in becoming a scientist or a lawyer when he grows up. Alvaro would like to be a biologist or a mathematician.

The children call their teachers Don (which means "Mr") followed by their first name. Nacho's class teacher is called Don José.

Who's in class?

There are both boys and girls at the school. Alvaro's class has 22 children and Nacho's has 18. In his class, Alvaro sits at the front on the left, near to the teacher. Nacho sits at the front of his class, too.

Lunchtime

The children eat lunch at around midday. Each class takes it in turn to eat in the school canteen. The school kitchen prepares fresh, healthy food every day. Lunch breaks in Spanish primary schools are often two hours long.

Lunch is paella and an omelette, with melon for dessert.

Nacho takes part in a relay race.

Sport

The boys go to football practice after school on Mondays and Wednesdays, and there's usually a match on Saturdays. During breaks, they play football, basketball, and *pilla-pilla* (catch) with their friends in the playground.

The boys have a football signed by the Real Madrid team.

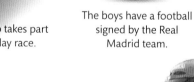

The boys are learning to play the recorder and the guitar at school.

Homework

The school day runs from 9:20 am to 4:30 pm, Monday to Friday. The boys do about two hours of homework every night. They have tests twice a week on Wednesdays and Fridays – once a month in English, and three times a month in science, maths, and Spanish.

Both boys have trial bikes, which they ride off-road in the countryside. In trial biking, riders have to navigate a very difficult course full of obstacles without allowing their feet to touch the ground.

"I would like to be a professional trial bike rider. You ride near rivers and rocks and in forests. You have to be very skilled."

41

Flora from Belgium

Flora is eight years old and lives in Brussels, the capital of Belgium. She has an older brother called Raphael. They go to an international school and their friends' families come from all over the world.

Coline has one white paw.

Flora loves everything to do with animals. She has a pet rabbit called Coline, who runs fast and sometimes bites.

Marketplace

Brussels has two official languages, French and Dutch, and all street signs are written in both languages. It is a market city, selling everything from birds and horses to flowers and food.

"I like my school a lot. It's special. But my favourite place is the playground."

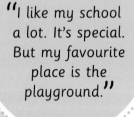

This horse is one of Flora's favourite toys. She hopes to have a real horse one day.

Flora and Raphael travel to school by bus. The bus stops at the end of their road at 7:30 am, and in winter it is still dark at that time. They take all the books they need for the day, carrying them in heavy bags.

Each day a child reads a thought for the day aloud and the children discuss it. Today's thought is: "Good design is making objects as beautiful as they are useful."

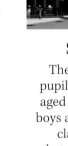

School for all

There are about 3,000 pupils in Flora's school aged from 5 to 18. Both boys and girls are in her class. Children wear what they like to school and they dress casually.

Working together

The children sometimes work in pairs. Here they are finding seven definitions from the dictionary. They have to use more than one dictionary to find the meanings of the more difficult words.

The children are making a timeline. It will show Earth's history from the first animals to the present day.

Tintin comes to school

Cartoon strips of Tintin and his faithful dog, Snowy, were drawn by a man called Hergé, who lived in Brussels. Scenes from the Tintin books decorate the entrance hall of the school.

Lunchtime

Students can choose either a vegetarian or a meat dish each day. It is put on their table and they serve themselves. Flora likes meat and vegetables, but she doesn't like fish.

Flora loves music and is learning the piano. She has been playing for six months.

Every evening Flora's parents help her to do at least one hour's homework.

Isabelle from the Netherlands

Isabelle is 11 years old and lives in Amsterdam, in the Netherlands. Her flat is close to the city-centre shops and museums. Each day she rides her bike to school along cycle paths that criss-cross the city.

Amsterdam is built on land that used to be part of the sea. Engineers built a network of canals that are still used today to transport goods and drain rainwater from the marshy land.

Isabelle's school

Isabelle's school is made up of three buildings that sit alongside canals. They are joined together by a playground. Isabelle's classroom is on the first floor.

Family life

Isabelle lives with her mum and dad in a two-bedroom flat. Her mum works in a bank and her dad teaches Indonesian martial arts.

Isabelle has a spelling and grammar test, then she works on fractions in a maths class. When the children have finished their work, they make themselves a cup of tea in the classroom if they want to.

Isabelle's teacher, Franz, is an enthusiastic musician who plays the guitar to his class. Isabelle and many of her friends are learning to play the guitar, too.

The art lesson

The children paint self-portraits, copying the style of the artist Picasso. They mix their colours in old egg boxes, which can be recycled afterwards.

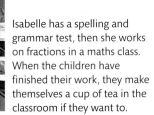

This is the Spanish artist Pablo Picasso.

Isabelle has painted herself from three different angles.

Isabelle's school does not have a kitchen. The children bring in food from home.

In bad weather the children stay inside and play games such as table football.

Most days Isabelle and her friends like to play basketball and football.

After school Isabelle goes to martial arts class with her dad.

Søren from Denmark

Søren goes to school in Vejen, a small town in Denmark. He is 10 years old and a keen footballer. He was named Søren after a famous footballer, Søren Lerby, who played for Bayern Munich and for Denmark.

Miniature Danish flags stand in the corner of Søren's classroom.

Cycling to school

Getting around

Cycling makes Søren quite independent. He travels to school along peaceful cycle paths, but there is one busy road he has to cross by himself. Søren has travelled all over Denmark to play in football matches with the local youth team. He hopes to become a professional footballer one day.

There are about 500 boys and girls aged 10 to 14 years at Søren's school.

Colourful carnival masks made by Søren and his classmates.

Learning

Søren's class studies English, history, and maths, with a different teacher for each subject. They get about half an hour's homework each night. Søren is currently doing a project about Albert Einstein, which involves many experiments.

In the library

There are a few computers in the school library, but not enough for every child, so they have to take turns.

The children play "Simon Says" in their English lesson. The length of the school day varies, but usually runs from 8 am to 1 pm. There is no school uniform and the children call the teachers by their first names.

Family life

Søren has a younger brother of 8, and two sisters of 12 and 14. The oldest is away at boarding school. When he is 14, Søren hopes to go to a boarding school that specializes in soccer.

The children gobble down their lunch quickly so they can go and play football for the rest of the lunch break. The girls play, too.

" I once went by myself to Copenhagen on the train. I played computer games. It was fine."

Søren has been playing the guitar for five years, and the piano for two.

The family adopted two stray cats.

44

Chiara from Italy

Rolling hills

Chiara's home town, Villa d'Adda, is about 30 km (20 miles) northeast of Milan, in the foothills of the Alps. The town is famous in Italy for its ferry, which is based on a drawing by Leonardo da Vinci.

Eleven-year-old Chiara has recently started secondary school. She lives in a town near Milan, Italy, and has two older brothers – one goes to a different school and the other has left school.

A bright mural decorates a school corridor. *Ciao* means both "hello" and "see you later."

A former monastery

The spacious school building, set in large grounds, has its own lake. It used to be a monastery. There are 28 children in Chiara's class – 14 girls and 14 boys, all aged 10 or 11. At the moment they are revising material they learned in primary school.

Chiara's class visits the school's chapel, which is quite grand. The children are still getting to know each other and learning to find their way around the school and its grounds.

Chiara only recently moved to this school. The children each sit at their own desk, with the desks usually arranged in a horseshoe shape.

Chiara loves bright colours.

The whole class is learning to play the recorder.

"I help Mum to clean the house and empty the dishwasher. I'm good because I listen to my mum."

At home

Chiara spends more than three hours a day on her homework. Her favourite subject is Italian literature.

Chiara's favourite toy is a tiny dog, which is only 5 cm (2 in) long.

Every Monday Chiara visits her grandparents for a lunch of home-cooked spaghetti and meatballs.

Family ties

Chiara's mother is a teacher and her father is a writer and journalist. Chiara's grandparents live nearby. She likes to go walking with them and their dog.

Chiara can ride a horse. She is learning to jump, starting with low poles and then building up.

She also enjoys playing on her swing, riding her bike, skateboarding, and taking country walks.

Fanny from Germany

Fanny is nine years old and lives with her parents, brother, and baby sister on the edge of a small village in southern Germany. Her school is 3.5 km (2 miles) away in a nearby town, and she travels there by bus.

Country setting

Fanny's village sits in flat farmland surrounded by small, rolling hills. Many of the roads have separate cycle paths.

Brother and sister

Fanny's brother, Felix, is seven years old and goes to school with Fanny. Their little sister, Lilly, is eight months old. Fanny thinks Lilly is sweet and likes to carry her around and read to her. When Lilly cries at night she wakes Fanny up.

Fanny likes reading books that are full of pictures.

This pony's legs bend forwards so it can lie down.

Bus to school

Each morning the bus picks up about 50 children and takes them to their school in Schwabhausen. Fanny's bus stop is across the road from her house. The bus drops the children outside school in time for an 8 am start.

Lessons last for 45 minutes. School finishes at 1 pm, when the children go home for lunch. Each day Fanny has an hour of homework, which she normally does right after lunch so that it is out of the way and she can play.

Modern building

Solar panels on the roof of the school building generate electricity to heat the classrooms. Inside it is light and bright, with the children's colourful artwork decorating the walls. There are 24 children in Fanny's class, aged eight or nine. Fanny is the oldest

Peg away

In maths, Fanny answers questions using mini clothes-pegs instead of writing the answers. Each colour represents a number. When she has finished, she turns over the page to check her answers on the back.

The children line up outside their classroom, ready for the day's lessons. Fanny shares a desk in the front row. Her favourite subjects are German, English, computers, choir, and crafts.

There is no school uniform and children usually wear trousers, t-shirts, and jumpers.

The class teacher is called Frau Schläbitz.

This shows windy weather.

This picture, on the door of the classroom, welcomes the children.

Music lesson

In music class, students sing and move to action songs. They play percussion instruments including tambourines and cymbals. Then they rehearse a musical they are performing at the end of term. Fanny loves to sing and is in the choir.

The class is working on a nature project.

This is a reminder of German grammar.

Students draw and colour in pictures when they learn about a subject.

In the gym

The children play a game of cat and mouse around a huge circular sheet. Then they split into groups in different activity areas. The groups spend five minutes on one activity before moving to the next.

Fanny swirls a long ribbon. She makes big circles and figures of eight.

Wobble boards are good for balance. There is a mat to land on if anyone falls.

Fanny holds onto a rope to help her climb a bench to the wall bars.

After school, Fanny and Felix play football on the grass behind their house.

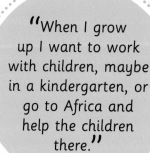

"When I grow up I want to work with children, maybe in a kindergarten, or go to Africa and help the children there."

Marek's walk to school takes him through the city along cobble streets and through tree-line parks. In the autumn the wal takes longer because Marek like to collect leaves and chestnut

> **"** I like walking through the leaves. **"**

Obwarzanki (bread rings) are a popular snack in the streets of Krakow.

The school was founded in 1871 and has been located in the same building since 1877.

Marek from Poland

Marek, who is eight years old, is from the centre of Krakow, one of Poland's major cities. He lives with his mother and father, and two cats called Szarak and Tunczyk, who sleep on Marek's bed at night. In the summer, the family visits Marek's grandmother in the countryside.

School day

Marek is in the second grade, where most of the lessons are taught by the same teacher. From the fourth grade, different subjects are taught by different teachers. Marek eats both lunch and dinner at school. After school he sometimes goes to dancing lessons. Once a week, he goes to scouts.

Work and play

Today the children are learning about the different jobs that people do. In the school library, the librarian tells them about her work. The children also visit the school secretary and the school cook.

This album is full of friendly messages from Marek's classmates.

Marek's best friends are Romek and Kacper.

Marek's class visits the park near the school. They play team games, passing a ring from person to person.

They collect fallen leaves and make pictures with them on the ground.

Europe

Celebrating autumn

Every term the school chooses a topic and the children learn about it. Last year it was Polish history, and this year it's ecology. The children are learning about the seasons and animals. Next term they will visit an organic farm.

The children are making pictures inspired by the shapes and colours of autumn.

First, each child draws a flower shape by tracing around a card template.

Then they cut out flower shapes, first in yellow and then again in orange paper.

Next, they cut out the leaves and stalks, this time using bright green paper.

Finally, they stick the pieces onto card, decorating the centre of the flowers with scrunched-up balls of tissue paper. Then each child signs his or her picture.

Marek prepares food for the cats.

"When I grow up I would like to be a vet because I like animals and I want to help them."

Singing is an enjoyable way to learn.

Religious studies

Every Tuesday, Marek attends religious studies classes at the family's church. He learns stories from the Bible and sings along to religious songs while his teacher plays the guitar.

Krakow is famous for the pigeons in the market square. Marek loves to stop and feed them.

Marek's song book

Asia

This is the largest of all the continents, with hugely varied landscapes and climates. Schools in China have existed for 3,000 years, India has one of the oldest school systems in the world, and Japanese children have been learning their characters since 500 BCE. So it's off to school!

Turkey

Turkey borders eight countries and two seas, and bridges two continents – Asia and Europe. It therefore has a unique blend of western and eastern traditions and culture.

Russia

Russia – the largest country in the world – spans Asia and Europe. Moscow is the capital city. At its centre stands St Basil's cathedral with its traditional Russian "onion" domes.

Mongolia

Mongolia is a land of rugged mountains, vast deserts, and dry, grassy plains called steppes. Here wandering tribes of nomads ride horses to herd livestock including camels, cattle, and goats.

Jordan

The ancient ruins of Petra are part of Jordan's long history. Some buildings in this unique city were carved into sheer rock and date back to Roman times.

Japan

Zoom! Super-express trains speed across the earthquake zones of Japan in high-tech splendour.

South Korea

One half of South Korea's population lives in or near Seoul, the buzzing capital and one of the biggest cities in the world.

Saint Petersburg
Panayevsk
Moscow
RUSSIA
Istanbul
KAZAKHSTAN
TURKEY
GEORGIA
CYPRUS
ARMENIA
AZERBAIJAN
LEBANON SYRIA
ISRAEL Amman
JORDAN IRAQ
UZBEKISTAN
TURKMENISTAN
ASIA
MONGOLIA
Kharkorin
KYRGYSTAN
TAJIKISTAN
CHINA
NORTH KOREA
JAPAN Chiba
Seoul SOUTH KOREA
KUWAIT
IRAN
AFGHANISTAN
Shanghai
SAUDI ARABIA
BAHRAIN
QATAR
U.A.E.
PAKISTAN
Mussoorie
Delhi
NEPAL
BHUTAN
TAIWAN
YEMEN OMAN
INDIA
BANGLADESH
MYANMAR (BURMA)
LAOS
VIETNAM
PHILIPPINES
THAILAND
CAMBODIA
SRI LANKA
BRUNEI
MALAYSIA
SINGAPORE
INDONESIA
Maliana
EAST TIMOR

Israel

Lying at the junction of three continents – Africa, Asia, and Europe – this small country is home to Jerusalem (above), a city holy to Judaism, Christianity, and Islam.

India

India has a population of more than 1.2 billion – almost four times that of the USA. The country is mainly farmland, and in the north is the highest mountain range in the world, the Himalayas.

China

China has the world's largest population – more than 1.3 billion people. It boasts the world's longest structure, the Great Wall of China (below).

East Timor

In 2002, East Timor became the first new country of the 21st century, after gaining independence from Indonesia. This small country, with 1.2 million people, has two official languages – Portuguese and Tetum.

Ksenia from Russia

Ksenia is 12 and lives in St Petersburg, in Russia. She goes to an Academy school. Here, more subjects are taught than in other state schools, including folklore, journalism, and languages.

St Petersburg was founded more than 300 years ago. It has grand buildings and canals, and was once the home of the Russian ruling family.

"When I grow up I'd like to work with people. Maybe I'll be a translator."

The school

Ksenia's school used to be a church. It doesn't have playing fields, but Ksenia doesn't mind as it has an indoor gym. The school hires security guards to check who comes into the building. They are paid for by parents.

Where to sit

Children mostly sit where they choose. Sometimes though, the teacher makes girls sit next to boys to stop children chatting. Ksenia doesn't think this works.

Working away

Ksenia has art lessons at school as well as at the Hermitage Museum nearby. In summer, the class stays at a monastery off the coast of St Petersburg, where they learn about the natural surroundings.

Ksenia's painting of trees

Olga from Russia

Olga is eight years old and goes to school in Moscow, in Russia. Olga is unable to walk and has to use a wheelchair. She goes to a regular school with nearly 400 other children from the city. Ramps have been built in the school so that Olga can travel around with ease.

Olga works hard in class and enjoys drawing and finding out about the stars and planets. At home she likes to watch the Russian cartoon character Cheburashka, a fairytale animal from a tropical rainforest. She would have her own real-life Cheburashka, if she could.

Alexei from Russia

Alexei is 10 years old and lives near Panayevsk, in the icy north of Russia. Alexei comes from reindeer-herding people called Nenets. Each year he spends three months with his family, then, as winter draws near, he travels to boarding school in a helicopter. He lives there for the next nine months.

Children look out of a helicopter window.

Taking flight

Children like Alexei first go off to boarding school when they are about seven. Helicopters are also used to deliver supplies and post. They can fly in temperatures well below freezing – only heavy snow or strong winds stop them.

Cold walk

As school is made up of several separate buildings, children have to walk across the frozen playground to go from one to another. They play outside in all but the most severe weather.

Today's lunch is steaming hot soup. Favourite foods include reindeer meat and fish.

Lassos are used to catch hold of reindeer. Alexei has one made from nylon.

A school day

Alexei has lessons on weekdays and Saturday mornings. He speaks Russian and the reindeer herders' language, Nenets. Nenets has many words to describe snow, reindeer breeding, hunting, and fishing.

Children go to bed at 9 pm and rise at 7 am. Usually 2–8 children share a room, sleeping under thick duvets.

"My friends are important to me. We do our homework all together at my house."

Aysima is 11 years old and lives with her family in Istanbul, Turkey. Her school overlooks the Bosphorus, a strip of water that flows through the city and separates Asia and Europe.

Aysima lives with her mother, father, and younger sister.

Breakfast

On school days Aysima eats cereal and fruit for breakfast. On weekends she has a breakfast of tomatoes, white cheese, olives, bread, and honey. This is washed down with strong black tea, called *çay*, diluted with hot water. Aysima's mother serves this in tulip-shaped glasses, first pouring in very strong tea from one pot, then diluting it with hot water from another.

Tea

Hot water

This is a Turkish mosque.

This is an Armenian church.

On the streets

Aysima travels to school by car or on the school bus. She doesn't like the busy rush-hour traffic because it holds her up and often makes her late for school.

In the evenings, Aysima packs her school bag with a text book and work book for each lesson the next day.

Aysima lives in a multicultural area of Istanbul, where mosques, churches, and synagogues are built close together. Both Armenian and Turkish children go to Aysima's school and both languages are spoken there.

Aysima at school

Aysima moved to her school a year ago. She already has lots of friends who visit her at home. Now that she is 11, she wears a grey and pink uniform. Up to the age of 10, the uniform is blue.

Old school

There are 34 students in Aysima's class. She feels very lucky because some schools in Turkey have 60 or more children in a class. Aysima's school building once belonged to Marko Pasha, a court official who lived around 150 years ago. He listened to people's complaints, and even today there is a saying in Turkey, "Go tell your problem to Marko Pasha".

Homework

Aysima lives high up in a block of flats. When the weather is good she does her homework on the balcony. There she can hear the mosques in the area making the call to prayer. She likes working on projects best, particularly ones on the Aegean region of Turkey and Greece. Aysima's favourite subjects are Turkish and English.

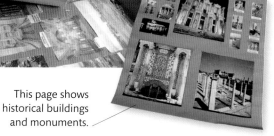

This page shows historical buildings and monuments.

Aysima made a frame for this picture of Istanbul.

This dance for the bride represents love, marriage, and the night before the wedding.

After school

Aysima's father is a volleyball instructor and Aysima likes to play volleyball after school. She is also planning to do a course in Turkish folk dancing. Every region has its own dances, with particular costumes, steps, and instruments. Some dances are only performed by women and girls.

Make it

Aysima loves to cook and often prepares food for her friends to eat. She also spends hours making things with beads, including jewellery, candle holders, and colourful slippers.

This is a bracelet.

These bead slippers are not for wearing.

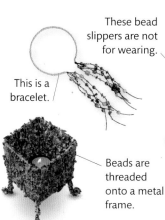

Beads are threaded onto a metal frame.

Ramadan

During the month of Ramadan, adult Muslims traditionally fast (do not eat) from dawn until dusk. Aysima goes to the baker to buy *iftar* bread, which she will share with her parents when they break their fast in the evening.

Dana with her cousin Rania, who is in the same class.

Dana from Jordan

Dana is 10 years old and lives in Amman, the capital of Jordan. She has an eight-year-old brother called Karam. The pair travel to their school by bus. The journey takes about 30 minutes.

School campus

Dana's school has a running track and a full-size, 400-seat theatre, which is also used by the local community. There are science laboratories and computer rooms as well. Dana's favourite subject is English. About 1,000 pupils attend her school.

Mixed lessons

Many pupils are Jordanian, but some come from elsewhere in the Middle East, Africa, and Europe. Lessons are in English and Arabic – most of the children are bilingual.

Special project

Dana's class is learning about the Solar System. The students have made a model of the planets and their orbits around the Sun.

Dana plays with her friends before school starts at 8 am. Classes end at 2:30 pm.

> "I want to be a designer or a famous actress when I leave school."

Dana with her parents and younger brother Karam.

Dana is a keen dancer. She takes ballet lessons twice a week and has been learning since she was four years old.

At home after school, Dana roller skates while Rania rides beside her on a scooter.

Yotam *from* Israel

Salam is Arabic for "peace".

Eleven-year-old Yotam lives in a village mid-way between Jerusalem and Tel Aviv, in Israel. Although Jewish and Arab people have fought over religion and territory in his country, Yotam goes to a mixed school, where children study together in harmony.

SIGND OF FRIENDSHIP

In the classroom

There are 26 children in Yotam's class, about the same number of girls as boys, all aged 11 or 12. The children don't wear a uniform, and they call their teachers by their first names. The children have language lessons in Hebrew, Arabic, and English. There are exams once a term.

The school promotes peace and friendship between Jewish and Arab people. A rainbow gate marks the entry to the playground.

Yotam looks forward to playtime, as he likes to run around with the other children.

Yotam is Jewish, while his friend Amir is a Palestinian Arab.

Special studies

Yotam's favourite lessons are music and sport. He is learning to play the recorder and the guitar. He also enjoys learning about medieval history, and collects historical figures.

Yotam likes working on his computer. He is currently designing a website.

He has about one hour of homework each night.

Deepak from India

Deepak is eight years old and lives with his mother, father, and ten-year-old brother, Atul, in Mussoorie, in the foothills of the Himalaya mountains in India. Deepak wants to do well at school and works hard. Each day he spends five hours there, then goes home and studies for another two to three hours. He hopes to become a scientist one day and discover a new planet.

Deepak

Atul

Deepak's family

Deepak lives on a rabbit farm, where his father works as the caretaker. Deepak's elder brother was born in the neighbouring country of Nepal. Then the family moved to India and Deepak was born. Deepak speaks Hindi and Nepali at home, and English at school.

For lunch Deepak eats flat, pan-fried bread called *paratha* with jam or pickles. Both his parents cook.

Deepak carries his lunch in metal pans that stack together. Metal clasps hold the lid on, and the handle folds down flat.

Deepak loves playing outdoors – climbing walls, cycling, and playing badminton. At home, he likes watching TV and playing with his favourite toy car.

Foot work

It takes Deepak, Atul, and their mother half an hour to walk to school each day. The boys have a bicycle, which they share, but they don't ride it to school. They go together with their mother, who is a helper at their school. She rings the bell at the end of classes.

High learning

Deepak's school is built from timber, stone, and brick, and sits high up on the hillside. Inside the building, the classrooms are arranged in a row with no corridor, so Deepak has to walk through lots of other classrooms to reach his own. His favourite subject is English. He also enjoys making things in craft classes.

Wild animals, including deer, wild boar, and leopards, live in the rocky hillside where Deepak goes to school. Deepak's mother has even seen a leopard in the trees near their house. Leopards usually leave people alone, but during hard winters they may steal farm animals.

A leopard's spotted coat acts as camouflage.

"I like Gandhi, who is called Bapu (Father). He helped us get freedom from the British."

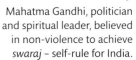

Mahatma Gandhi, politician and spiritual leader, believed in non-violence to achieve *swaraj* – self-rule for India.

Good citizens

Each morning, the children line up to sing the national anthem before they file into class. One of Deepak's favourite lessons is moral science, where he learns how to help people in need. He is glad that children from any religion are allowed to study at his school. If students misbehave, they have to stand on a bench and hold up their hands.

Question time

Deepak has exams four times a year and short tests all the year round. During morning assembly, students read the day's newspapers and answer questions on current news and general knowledge. They call their teacher "ma'am".

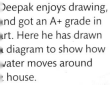

Deepak enjoys drawing, and got an A+ grade in art. Here he has drawn a diagram to show how water moves around a house.

Water moves downwards because of the force of gravity.

In the playground, Deepak drinks water overflowing from a tank that is filled from mountain springs. Water is collected from melting snow on the hilltops. It runs into pipes and down to farms and houses. Any unused water trickles out of the pipes to feed the vegetation.

"I wish for getting very good marks in my exams."

There are 19 children in Deepak's class, including five girls. Deepak likes girls, although most of his friends are boys.

Sumandhara from India

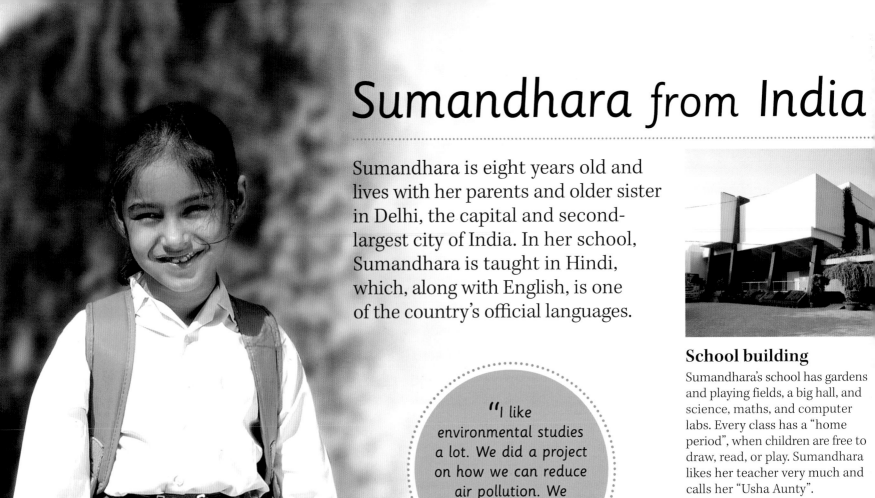

Sumandhara is eight years old and lives with her parents and older sister in Delhi, the capital and second-largest city of India. In her school, Sumandhara is taught in Hindi, which, along with English, is one of the country's official languages.

"I like environmental studies a lot. We did a project on how we can reduce air pollution. We should plant more trees.**"**

School building

Sumandhara's school has gardens and playing fields, a big hall, and science, maths, and computer labs. Every class has a "home period", when children are free to draw, read, or play. Sumandhara likes her teacher very much and calls her "Usha Aunty".

Sumandhara's ID badge shows her name, her class, and who to call if she is hurt or ill.

Sumandhara likes drawing. She prefers it to studying.

Sumandhara wears a school uniform – girls can choose between trousers and skirts. Sumandhara likes the nursery class best because the children there can wear any clothes they like.

These are Sumandhara's crayons. She also has coloured pencils. Her favourite colour is pink.

Abhinandan

Children and teachers greet everybody by waving their hands. They call it *abhinandan*. They also wave to say "thank you" and to applaud. It is their way of reducing noise at school.

Sumandhara plays with her friends on the bus to school.

The children share desks and change places on Tuesdays.

Students use building blocks to solve maths problems.

Children love to play during lunch break and games peric

Reena from India

Reena is eight years old and lives in Noida, a satellite town of Delhi in northern India. Reena stays at home during the day to look after her younger sister, Santoshi, and does chores such as washing and cooking. She also enjoys drawing and watching television. She goes to school at night.

This is the entrance to Reena's night school.

Reena practises her numbers on the blackboard. This is made from a kind of flexible plastic that can be rolled and stacked in a corner.

"My parents are planning to enrol me in a day school but I don't know when they will be able to do it. I don't mind staying at home."

A school night

Reena goes to school from 7:30 pm until 9 pm. Boys go there from 9 pm onwards. Reena is learning her alphabet. She knows how to add up but cannot subtract yet.

Family life

Reena lives with her family in a one-room brick house. Her father paints houses and her mother works as a stonemason at building sites. Reena has one brother and four sisters. Her eldest sister is married.

It takes two minutes to walk through the alleys to school.

There are no desks or chairs, but the carpet is soft and dry.

Volunteers teach everyone, from toddlers to adults.

Reena enjoys night school as she loves to learn new things.

Xinpei from China

Xinpei is six years old and lives in southwest China. Her parents are farmers, and in the countryside where Xinpei lives, school is often a long way from a child's home. However, a new school has been built 5 km (3 miles) from Xinpei's house, so she goes to school there.

Journey to school

Xinpei walks to school with friends from her village. On the way they play and pick flowers. They cross a flood wall that stops the river from damaging farmland during the rainy season. It takes an hour and a half to get to school.

Catching a ride

During bad weather, parents drive all the local children to school. They operate a relay system, taking one group of children, then going back for the next.

Until 2016, couples in China were only allowed to have one child to stop the country's population from growing too fast. As Xinpei's parents live in the countryside, they were allowed to have a second child. He is called Xinwang.

Xinpei arrives at school early and plays hula-hoop with her friends before class starts at 8 am. This hula-hoop belongs to the school. Xinpei dreams that one day she will own one herself.

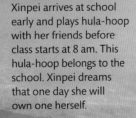

A school day

Each Monday, the whole school stands to attention while the national anthem is played over a loudspeaker and the national flag is hoisted up the flagpole. The headmaster makes a speech.

Two to a desk

Children sit in pairs and keep their books inside their desks. They study many things, including Chinese, maths, and music. Although going to school is free, parents are usually expected to pay for essentials such as books and pencils. These can be too expensive for poor families, so some children are not sent to school. However, in Xinpei's school, these things are free.

This picture by Xinpei is called *In spring and autumn time*. The ducks live on the pond by Xinpei's house.

It's eye time

Every day the class performs 10 minutes of eye exercises to music. These are designed to relax the eyes and protect eyesight. The children look up and down and side to side. Then they gently massage around their eyes, stimulating special places called acupressure points, which are important in Chinese medicine.

Time to eat

There is no canteen in the school, so children take packed lunches of cold rice and vegetables. They can eat these in the classrooms if it rains. One day Xinpei forgot to take her lunch to school so two of her friends shared their food with her.

Home work

The children have to tidy their classrooms and sweep the floor before they go home at 3:30 pm. After school, children pick tea. They work quickly, their small hands easily plucking the newest and tiniest leaves. In one hour, a child can earn enough to buy a packet of sweets.

The whole school exercises in the playground each day. The school has a new uniform, but children only wear it on special occasions. Children wear red scarves if they are members of the Young Pioneers of China.

In music class, the teacher plays the tune *Frère Jacques* on the piano. The children sing words from a popular rhyme: "Two tigers, two tigers, running fast, running fast, one has no eyes, one has no tail, it's very strange, it's very strange."

Yiting from China

Ten-year-old Yiting and her mother leave their home in Shanghai at 7 am for the short walk to school, past a playground and a toy shop. Yiting has no brothers or sisters, but she usually plays with a friend after school.

My class

Yiting's class has 23 girls and 7 boys. There are 750 children aged 7 to 11 at the school. The school building is about 100 years old and very distinctive.

Hard at work

The school day lasts from 7:15 am to 4:15 pm, five days a week. Yiting calls her teacher "*Zhang Laoshi*" (Teacher Zhang). She sits at the back of the class as she is quite tall.

School clothes

Most of the time the children wear their own clothes, but on Mondays they wear uniform for the national flag-raising ceremony.

Yiting's class rehearse for a dance performance in a couple of weeks' time.

Yiting demonstrates a chess move at the front of the class.

Chess lessons

Chess is often taught as an after-school activity at schools in China, but Yiting's school is particularly well-known for its pupils' achievements in chess competitions. The children have a chess class once a week for 45 minutes.

Yiting and her classmates coax their hoops along with sticks at break time.

Balancing on a wobble board is also a favourite playground activity at Yiting's school.

Yiting's favourite class is physical education, and she also loves playing outside.

Jiyu from China

…u's school building

Jiyu is nine years old. He lives in Zhu Jia Jiao, a town about 35 km (20 miles) west of Shanghai, and walks to school. There are 40 children in each class and Jiyu shares a desk with his best friend. When he grows up, he would like to be the best teacher in town.

Jiyu has a 20-minute walk to school.

After school, the children stay for a session of papercutting, an ancient Chinese art form.

…ye exercises

…vice a day, during the morning and afternoon …reaks, the children perform a series of eye exercises. …hile listening to soft music, they are guided through …ur different moves that help their eyes to relax.

Papercutting requires patience and care.

Children record their activities on a board.

Uniform

All the children wear the school uniform of a tracksuit. The boys' tracksuit is navy blue, while the girls' is red. The red scarf represents the Chinese flag.

…u plays *ti jian zi*, a shuttlecock game …at is a little like badminton, but played …th…out a racquet.

The aim is to keep a shuttlecock in the air for as long as possible just by kicking it.

Jiyu is learning to play the *erhu*, a traditional Chinese musical instrument.

Hassa from Mongolia

Hassa is 10 years old and lives in Kharkorin, in Mongolia. His mother died when he was born, so during the week he lives with his older sister, and at weekends his grandmother looks after him. Hassa goes to two different schools – a modern school, and a monastery school where he is training to be a Buddhist monk.

At the monastery, Hassa wears a long, loose gown called a *del*. It is held in place with a sash.

Home life

Hassa and his 18-year-old sister live in a traditional tent called a *ger*. It has a wooden frame covered with two layers of thick felt fabric, which also covers the floor. Most of Hassa's family are nomadic herders, which means they move around to find fresh pastures for their animals.

Hassa likes watching films at home. His favourite film is *Shrek* and his favourite toy is this Shrek model.

Home cooking

Hassa's sister cooks on a stove in the middle of the *ger*. Smoke from the stove escapes through a hole in the roof.

The school

Many children from nomadic herding families go to boarding schools, but as Hassa lives with his sister during term time, he goes to a day school. The school has two sittings, one in the morning and one in the afternoon. Hassa goes in the afternoon, from 2 pm to 6 pm. There is no running water at Hassa's school, so children have to use an outside toilet and clean their hands on antiseptic wipes.

Good student

Hassa likes school and keeps up with his homework. In Mongolia, most children start school at six or seven years old. Hassa started school after a year at the monastery. He is a year older than his classmates.

In the classroom

There are more girls than boys in Hassa's class because some of the boys are at home helping their fathers look after the animals. The girls are at school so they can be educated, get good jobs, and take their wages home to their families. Most of the children wear school uniform, and girls decorate their hair with pink netting bows.

Time to eat

Hassa takes a bread roll for lunch. The school provides a drink made from raisins, which Hassa sips from a bowl.

Hassa's class teacher serves the children.

Hassa speaks Mongolian, which is written left to right using the 33 letters of the Cyrillic alphabet.

"I will go full-time to the monastery school when I am 13. Then I'll become a Buddhist monk."

At weekends, Hassa goes to the monastery where he trains to be a Buddhist monk, called a *lama*.

The *lamas* sit at low desks as they study nature and the Tibetan language. They also chant prayers.

As well as being ridden, horses provide meat. A mare's milk is fermented to make an alcoholic drink called *airag*.

After school

At weekends and during school holidays, Hassa stays in the country *ger* belonging to his grandmother. Hassa helps look after the family's 00 sheep, oxen, and horses. Four times a year, Hassa helps take down the *ger* and move it to fresh grazing land.

Hassa and his grandmother collect dried animal dung to burn on the fire.

Sun-Woo from South Korea

South Korea is a mountainous and hilly nation tucked between China and Japan. Most people in South Korea live in a city – more than 10 million in Seoul.

Six-year-old Sun-Woo comes from Seoul, the capital of South Korea, where she lives with her parents and younger sister. In most elementary schools and kindergartens in South Korea, children wear clothes of their own choice. However, Sun-Woo goes to a private school and wears school uniform.

City lights

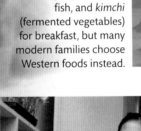

Sun-Woo and her family live in a modern apartment overlooking Seoul. Here, she stands at their big picture window with the lights of the city glittering behind her.

School run

Sun-Woo's school is close to her home, but it takes 20 minutes to drive there in the city's heavy traffic. In the mornings, her father drops her off on the way to the furniture store he owns.

Traditionally, Korean people eat rice, fish, and *kimchi* (fermented vegetables) for breakfast, but many modern families choose Western foods instead.

At school

Sun-Woo likes all her subjects, but English is her favourite. Each week she goes to the school forum (an open meeting) where children decide on one positive activity. Once they all agreed to be extra polite to their teachers.

Textbooks are labelled with the name of the child they belong to.

White shoes are part of Sun-Woo's uniform. When she gets to school, she takes them off, puts them in a cubbyhole, and goes to lessons wearing slippers.

Sun-Woo's school notebook

The children form an orderly line to walk between classrooms

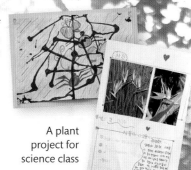

One of Sun-Woo's paintings

A plant project for science class

"My heroes are my parents. My greatest wish is for my family to be happy."

place to learn

here are 30 pupils in Sun-Woo's class – 16 boys and 14 girls. he teacher is called Chae Mi-Jung. Sun-Woo, who is not ry tall, sits at the front so she can see.

In Sun-Woo's school, there is a special classroom where the computers are kept.

Iaking music

ometimes in their music class, Sun-Woo nd her friends learn how to play a aditional Korean drum, called a *jangu*. It oks like an hourglass lying on its side.

Sun-Woo works hard to make one of the small, black, highly decorated hats that form part of Korean national dress.

Time to eat

All the children at Sun-Woo's school have lunch in the canteen. Each child has a separate tray and eats with chopsticks. Today, the menu includes rice and fish, with a fresh satsuma for dessert.

Fans are an important part of Korean costume. Like antique fans, Sun-Woo's are adorned with flowers.

Sun-Woo's finished hat is covered with brightly coloured ribbons and shapes.

The traditional Korean costume is called the *hanbok*. Very similar for men and women, it consists of a long, simple skirt or trousers, and a short jacket. Today, the *hanbok* is worn only for special celebrations. Sun-Woo's teacher helps the children in her class to learn about Korean history, culture, and traditions like this one.

Sun-Woo and her friends love to play hand-clapping games.

Sun-Woo loves the martial art of *taekwondo* and goes to classes three times a week.

Family mealtime

Food plays a very important part in Korean family life. Every day, Sun-Woo and her family try to sit down together to eat and exchange news.

Momona from Japan

Chiba's houses and factories sit on the long coastline of Tokyo Bay. The people who live there work in industries such as chemical production, fishing, and seaweed harvesting.

Kae

Momona

Momona and her friend, Kae, ride unicycles (cycles with one wheel). Momona can also ride a bicycle.

Momona is eight years old and lives in the city of Chiba, on the eastern coast of Japan. Her home is on the fifth floor of a large block of flats. She shares it with her mother, father, and younger sister and brother. Each day she takes the lift to the ground, then walks with her friends to the nearby school.

Momona and her friend, Saaya, head off to school.

In the morning

Momona reads the children's section of the newspaper to find out about other children around the world. Then she leaves for school. There is an artificial stream outside her flat that she likes to jump over.

School building

There are more than 600 children in Momona's school. The school has a library, gym, and outdoor swimming pool. In Momona's class, the children learn how to grow flowers and vegetables. Recently they grew sweet potatoes. Then they dug up, cooked, and ate them.

Shoe swap

There are rows and rows of cubbyholes at the entrance to Momona's school. This is where Momona changes into her white indoor shoes, called *uwabaki*.

Keeping fit

The children exercise in the large playground next to the school. They stretch, run, and climb on bars set up outside. Momona is very flexible and enjoys keeping fit. For P.E. classes, children change into comfortable shorts and tops.

Children warm up by stretching.

Class work

Momona sits at the front of the class where she has clear view. Momona likes school very much. Her favourite subjects include Japanese and music.

Serving each other

The children work in teams, taking turns to serve their classmates. They say *itadakimasu* – a prayer of thanks for their food. Then they settle down to eat in their classroom.

> "I want to be a kindly nursery school teacher and comfort small children when they cry."

Lunch is tuna and rice, eaten using chopsticks. Momona drinks milk with this.

At school, children work in pairs on the computer, taking turns to use the mouse.

Clean sweep

Before she goes home, Momona and the other children clean the classroom. They wash and polish the floors, wipe the windows and lockers, and clean the sinks and toilets. Momona likes having a clean classroom.

Children all over Japan love Hello Kitty toys. Momona also loves her robotic dog. She would like to have a real dog one day.

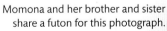

Music lessons

Each week after school, Momona has a piano lesson. The teacher lives in Momona's block of flats and Momona goes to her home for classes.

Momona is learning about musical notes and practises writing them in her book.

At home

Momona and her four-year-old sister, Ririka, love making origami animals from paper. They made these frogs. When it is bedtime, the children unroll their mattresses, called futons, and sleep on them. The whole family sleeps in the same room.

Momona and her brother and sister share a futon for this photograph.

Junivio *from* East Timor

Junivio is 10 years old and lives in Maliana in East Timor, one of the poorest countries in Asia. His home has no electricity and there is no postal service to deliver letters. Junivio walks to the only school in the area, which is 20 minutes away.

This is Lorinko, Junivio's pet parrot.

Grandpa   Mum   Dad

In the family

Junivio lives with his mother, father, and grandfather. He has five brothers and sisters, and many cousins. Junivio also has a dog called Bonja, named after an Indian film star.

Junivio with his brothers and cousin

Hot walk

Junivio walks past his favourite mountain every day on his way to school. He walks with his 11-year-old twin sisters, Lenah and Diana. Junivio wears his shirt outside his shorts because this helps him to keep cool in the hot and humid climate.

Class action

About 1,000 children go to Junivio's school, which is made up of three separate buildings. Junivio has classes in the afternoons, from 1 pm to 5 pm. His favourite subject is maths.

After school, Junivio plays chase with his brothers and sisters.

Junivio's sister and cousin cool down in a nearby stream.

The children work in groups guided by their head teacher. They are looking forward to the school getting its first computer.

In class

There are 32 children in Junivio's class. They speak a mixture of the local language, Tetum, and Portuguese. Students wear either the blue school uniform or their usual clothes from home. Junivio likes everything about school and enjoys learning about new things.

Make it

Children do not make many craft projects because the school has little money to pay for materials. However, Junivio's friend did make this drum from cardboard and coloured paper.

This drum makes a quiet thudding sound.

Junivio is making a "number square" up to 100 so he can look for patterns in numbers.

Fix it

Junivio likes to take things apart and rebuild them. He spends hours working on his bike.

These spanners are from Junivio's tool kit.

"When I'm older I hope I can be a mechanic. I like working with tools and assembling things."

Working at home

At home, Junivio practises maths on his blackboard. He has one hour of homework each night. As there is no electricity at his home, he has to do it before the sun sets, or by candlelight.

Home cooking

Junivio's mother is a school teacher. She also makes lovely cakes and doughnuts dusted with icing sugar. Her kitchen, at the back of the house, has a roof but no walls. Junivio helps by collecting sticks for her wood-burning stove.

Team sports are not taught during lesson time at school, but the children play football during breaks. At home, Junivio plays with boys from his village on the local football pitch. The village men hold football matches here every week.

Children jump and dive into the water where it is a bit deeper.

The stream is a place to play, wash, and clean clothes.

Australasia

Australasia consists of Australia, New Zealand, and several neighbouring South Pacific islands. For the most part, teaching in Australia and New Zealand is in English, and schools are similar to European schools. At the same time, both countries have also developed schools where the language and traditions of the original population are taught.

This is Australasia

Australian kangaroo

The kangaroo is a symbol of Australia. As tall as a man, this vegetarian browser can really hop – up to 3 m (10 ft) high.

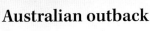

PALAU

Australian outback

The vast centre of Australia, called the outback, consists of dry bushlands. Uluṟu (above) is in the Northern Territory. The huge slab of sandstone rock of which Uluṟu is made formed about 500 million years ago and continues for about 5–6 km (3–4 miles) underground.

MICRONESIA

Rafting, New Zealand

Many New Zealanders enjoy adventure, like trips into the wilderness, bungy jumping, and white-water rafting (above). They also enjoy more traditional sports – rugby union is the national sport, and cricket and netball are also popular.

Sydney, Australia

The sail shapes of the Sydney Opera House are world famous. Sydney is the most populated city in Australia. It is a harbour city and has many beautiful beaches.

PAPUA NEW GUINEA

SOLOMON ISLANDS

○Yirrkala

VANUATU

FIJI

SAMOA

NEW CALEDONIA
(To France)

TONGA

A U S T R A L I A

A U S T R A L A S I A

Kiwi, New Zealand

The animal life in New Zealand is unique and exotic. It includes the kiwi bird – the national emblem of New Zealand.

Islands of New Zealand

There are two main islands, North and South, and the landscape ranges from craggy coastlines and long, sandy beaches to ancient forests and snow-capped mountains.

Turangi ○

NEW ZEALAND

Great Barrier Reef, Australia

This is the greatest coral reef system in the world. It is so big that it can be seen from space. It supports amazingly varied sea life including turtles, humpback whales, sharks, clownfish, sea snakes, and giant clams.

Gapirri *from Australia*

Nine-year-old Gapirri lives in Yirrkala, Arnhem Land, in the Northern Territory of Australia. He lives with his father, two sisters, and two brothers. The community of less than 1,000 people is famous for producing traditional Aboriginal art.

Aboriginal people have lived in Yirrkala since before historical records began.

Graham   Gloria   Rita   Aaron   Timmy

Aboriginal people use different names for different situations. It's common to use an Aboriginal name inside the community and a European name outside.

Yirrkala has a tropical climate and is warm all year round. Gapirri spends a lot of time on the beach.

SCHOOL

Cyclone-proof school

The school building has a modern look and is decorated with original works of art. It has been built to withstand a cyclone. Boys and girls are taught in separate classes.

Gapirri makes his way between the trees on the short walk to school.

Classes

Gapirri is in grade four at school. Attendance is encouraged but not compulsory, so in order to appeal to the children, lessons are informal, practical, and often take place outdoors. The children like to learn this way.

Lessons are in Yolngu, the local language. Classes generally run from 8:30 am to 3 pm, Monday to Friday.

Gapirri plays the drums and sings with his friends in a band. They practise at school, but they don't have a name yet.

Playing basketball

Australian rules football is popular, too.

Practical skills

The children often go on outings in the school bus. They practise archery in the bush. Most days, Gapirri also goes hunting with his father, Timmy, a ranger.

"When we do corroboree (traditional dancing) I put white colour on my face. It comes from a rock. You get a stick and crush it up and mix it with water."

The beach

From his house, Gapirri can see the sea. He once saw a crocodile at the beach. School outings to a water hole or the beach are a chance to go fishing and swimming. Gapirri also goes to the beach with his father, who is teaching him how to spear, cook, and eat turtles. He's interested in becoming a ranger like his dad when he grows up.

Playtime

Imagine having this as your local playground! On outings from school, the children are taught to play safely. Gapirri and his friends love diving for shells.

Parekaawa from New Zealand

Parekaawa is 10 years old and lives in Turangi, in a volcanic region of New Zealand's North Island. Parekaawa is a member of the native Maori community and attends a bilingual school, where both Maori and English are taught as well as Maori culture and traditions.

Family way

Parekaawa lives with her mother, father, and younger brother, Arekatera, near the shores of New Zealand's largest lake, Lake Taupo. Parekaawa was named after a Maori princess by her grandmother and a close aunt.

In cooking, flax leaves are wrapped around raw food. The parcel is lowered into a hole over hot rocks and a damp cloth is placed on top to make steam. Five hours later, the food is ready.

Parekaawa plaits flax leaves to make flowers called *puti-puti*.

Flax flower

Nature walks

Some mornings, Parekaawa, Arekatera, and their dad go for walks to look at the hot volcanic pools and steaming streams that surround their home. In the forest they collect flax leaves, which they use in a traditional way of cooking.

School time

School starts at 8:30 am. Parekaawa travels there on a bus that sometimes breaks down. She and her friends wear a uniform with a swirling pattern on one side that represents local plant life. The triangle on the school badge is a mountain.

Light touch

In class, Parekaawa learns about Maori carved totems, called *poupou*. Parekaawa's teacher says that to enjoy and understand a carving properly, people have to look at it with their eyes open, then feel it with their eyes closed.

This is Parekaawa's father with her mother in his arms. The other figure is Arekatera.

Australasia

rekaawa calls her teacher *"Whaea Liz"*. *haea* means "auntie" or "elder".)

Children help each other see and feel the carvings.

This carving is a junior boys' canoe-paddling trophy.

Parekaawa designs her own carving. It represents her family.

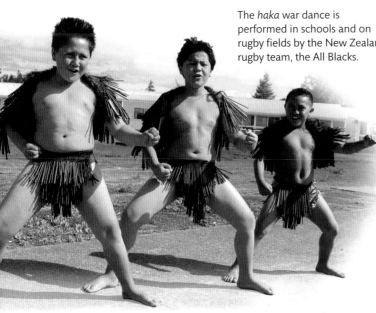

The *haka* war dance is performed in schools and on rugby fields by the New Zealand rugby team, the All Blacks.

"I would like to be a TV producer or an editor when I grow older."

Traditional dancing

On special occasions children perform traditional Maori dances. The girls perform the *poi*, where they spin string balls in circles, and the boys perform the *haka*.

At Brownies, Parekaawa cools off on a water slide. Water pours from a hose over a plastic sheet. Washing-up liquid makes it slippery.

Outside school, Parekaawa keeps busy kicking a football, playing the piano, and going to a nearby Brownies club for girls.

Parekaawa sits under a tree with her dad. She likes living near the lake and mountains. In summer she swims in the lake. In winter she goes skiing with her school.

Index

A
academy school 52
after-school club 32, 33, 48
animals 11, 20, 21, 24, 25, 42, 44, 45, 48, 51, 59, 66, 67, 72, 74, 75, 77
animal care 15, 49, 67
arts and crafts 15, 16, 19, 21, 23, 29, 39, 41, 43, 47, 49, 52, 55, 59, 63, 65, 73, 77, 79
Australia 74, 75, 76–77

B
baseball 20, 21
basketball 15, 19, 41, 43, 77
Belgium 35, 42
blackboard 31, 33, 61, 73
boarding school 26
Botswana 25, 32–33
Brazil 9, 12–13
breaktime 11, 15, 19, 41, 60, 64, 73
Buddhism 66–67

C
Canada 9, 22–23
chess 64
China 50, 51, 62–63, 64, 65
church 19, 49, 54
collecting water 17, 32
collecting wood 73
computers 12, 13, 16, 19, 26, 36, 57, 71, 73
cooking 11, 17, 21, 31, 61, 66
cricket 26, 36
cycling 18, 41, 44, 45, 70

DE
dancing 13, 35, 55, 56, 79
Day of the Dead 15
Denmark 35, 44
drum 12, 73, 77
East Timor 51, 72–73
Egypt 25, 28–29
England 35, 36
erhu 65
Ethiopia 25, 30–31
eye exercises 63, 65

FG
fishing 23, 77
flag 19, 62
football (soccer) 15, 20, 23, 26, 33, 37, 41, 43, 44, 47, 73
Australian rules 77
France 35, 38–39
Gandhi 59
Germany 46–47
Greek Orthodox Christianity 19
guitar 36, 39, 41, 43, 57

HI
headscarf 28, 30
helicopter 53
history 44, 57
homework 13, 16, 23, 29, 39, 41, 42, 46, 54, 55, 57
India 51, 58–59, 60, 61
Ireland 35, 37
Israel 51, 57
Italy 35, 45

JL
jangu 69
Japan 51, 70–71
Jordan 51, 56

language 10, 12, 13, 22, 23, 25, 33, 37, 51, 53, 56, 57, 73, 78
laundry 11, 61
library 44, 49

M
Market Day 26
maths 17, 19, 31, 33, 44, 47, 60, 73
Mexico 9, 14–15, 16–17
Mongolia 51, 66–67
mosque 54
mountain 10, 35, 51, 58, 72, 75
music lessons 19, 47, 63
Muslim 30

N
nature 11, 17, 36, 37, 47, 49, 52, 60, 78
Netherlands 35, 43
New Zealand 74, 75, 78–79
night school 61

PR
pencils 38, 63
Peru 9, 10–11
piano 20, 42, 71
Poland 35, 48–49
recorder 41, 45, 57
religious studies 49
Russia 51, 52–53

S
samba 12
school bus 13, 23, 37, 46, 56, 60
science 16, 23, 31, 41
shoes 68, 70
snowmobile 22
social studies 33
South Africa 24, 25, 26–27
South Korea 51, 68–69
Spain 34, 35, 40–41
sports lessons (PE) 13, 15, 29, 71
swimming 15, 19, 26, 37, 77

TU
tests 39, 43, 59
tidying up 45, 61, 71
Turkey 51, 54–55
uniform 14, 19, 23, 26, 33, 36, 40, 44, 55, 63, 64, 65, 66, 67, 68, 69, 78
USA 9, 18–19, 20–21

VW
violin 21
walking 20, 23, 27, 28, 30, 32, 36, 48, 58, 61, 62, 64, 65, 70, 72
washing up 17, 27, 33
whiteboard 14, 36

Acknowledgements
Dorling Kindersley would like to thank Polly Goodman for proofreading.

Thanks also to: Jay Goulden, Astrid Huerta Guevara, Care Huaraz (Peru), Jose Claudio Barros, Gilza Lopes Silveira de Mello, Priscilla Valdes, Patricia Magrini (Brazil), Gabriela Lopez Soria, Maria Cristina Galván Montero, Martin Furntes Chávez, Dr Felipe Bracho Carpizo, María Elena Guerra y Sánchez, Conafe (Mexico), FIRST AIR, Kativik School Board (Canada), Clare and Tony Green (South Africa), Gina Fubini (Italy), Piotr Pininski (Poland), Inna Yakovleva (Russian Federation), Seda Darcan Ciftci (Turkey), AID-Delhi (India), Mr Chen Haiwen, Mr Cui Xinhua (China), Hazel Benyon, The Venerable Baasansuren, VSO office Ulaanbaatar (Mongolia), In-Joon Chung (South Korea), Mark Harris (East Timor), Timmy Burarrwanga (Australia). Also thanks to Ed Merritt for cartography.

The publisher would like to thank the following for their kind permission to reproduce their photographs:
(Key: a-above; b-below/bottom; c-centre; f-far; l-left; r-right; t-top)

123RF.com: foottoo 8tl, Alexey Kuznetsov 51ftl; **Alamy Images:** AA World Travel Library 46tr; Karin Duthie 32tl; Chad Ehlers 51cr; Julio Etchart 51br; Gavin Hellier 25ca; Art Kowalsky 35tl (Ireland); Hideo Kurihara 51cra; Chris McLennan 52tr; Chris Pancewicz 35br; Photo Japan 71fcrb; Sepp Puchinger 30tl; Robert Harding Picture Library Ltd 25cra, 27tr (strawberry farm); Neil Setchfield 34cb (Tintin); Makoto Watanabe/MIXA Co., Ltd 70tl; White Star / Monica Gumm 35fcrb; Anthony Wiles 35cl; **Bryan and Cherry Alexander Photography:** 53br, 53cr, 53crb, 53fcrb, 53l, 53tr, 53tr (children); **Corbis:** Jon Arnold/JAI 28tl; Tom Bean 9clb; Morton Beebe 9br; Bettmann 59tr; Dean Conger 51bc; Richard du Toit 26tr; Beat Glanzmann 9tl (dog sleigh); Chris Hellier 55cr; Joson 9cla; Bodh Kharbu 51bl; Wayne Lawler/ Ecoscene 76tr; Charles & Josette Lenars 75ca; Gideon Mendel 26ca (Nelson Mandela); Joseph Sohm/Visions of America

18tl; Paul A. Souders 25cr; Hubert Stadler 10tr; Eberhard Streichan 35fbr; Torleif Svensson 25br; Patrick Ward 40tl; Julia Waterlow/Eye Ubiquitous 28br; **Flickr.com:** mrfysla1 54c; taminator 9tr (ice hockey); **Getty Images:** altrendo travel 75br; Gary Bell 75bl; Ram Shergill 35fbl; VisionsofAmerica/Joe Sohm 38tr; **Photolibrary:** Charles Bowman/Robert Harding Picture Library Ltd 68tl; **PunchStock:** Brand X Pictures 9fcra; Digital Vision 25bl; Alenda Svirid 52bc, 52br

All other images © Dorling Kindersley
For further information see: **www.dkimages.com**

And an extra big thanks to all the schools, staff, families, and especially the children, who appeared in
A School Like Mine.
Thank you, everyone.